Praise for *Thy Q*
from the Pat~~iurchy to Save Your Soul~~

"Kyndall Rothaus tells stories of the truth, power, courage, and grit of the women we so often have ignored because of the ways the dominant system works. These often-forgotten women of the Bible help us more clearly see the need for stories that make a profound break with the dominant system, the kind of spirituality that stewards the logic of liberation."

—Robyn Henderson-Espinoza, founder of the Activist
Theology project and author of *Activist Theology*

"Honest and liberating, *Thy Queendom Come* invites us to be citizens in a land like no other. Smashing the patriarchy has never been more life-giving."

—Karoline M. Lewis, author of *She: Five Keys
to Unlock the Power of Women in Ministry*

"Rothaus skillfully reinvigorates the voices and counter-narratives of women in biblical text and urges us to explore a new way of being within ourselves and in the world—one that centralizes healing, truth, and awake-ness for both the silenced and the silencer."

—Dr. Katie Lauve-Moon, author of *Preacher Woman* and
assistant professor at Texas Christian University

"Honest. Open. Probing. Embracing: This book offers *HOPE* for the queendom."

—Phyllis Trible, author of *God and the
Rhetoric of Sexuality* and *Texts of Terror*

"Rothaus offers a healing balm to our wounds of patriarchy, replacing our pain with power. *Thy Queendom Come* will leave you with chills, the hair on your arms standing on end."

—Rev. Aurelia Dávila Pratt, lead pastor and a founder of Peace of Christ Church and cohost of the *Nuance Tea* podcast

"If Christianity is to be transformed, this is a way forward."

—Carol P. Christ, author of *Goddess and God in the World* and leader of Goddess Pilgrimage to Crete

Thy Queendom Come

Salvatrix Mundi, by Lisbeth Cheever-Gessaman
(She Who Is Art)

Thy Queendom Come

BREAKING FREE FROM THE PATRIARCHY TO SAVE YOUR SOUL

KYNDALL RAE
ROTHAUS

BROADLEAF BOOKS
MINNEAPOLIS

To my daughters.
May they be fully themselves,
unencumbered by patriarchal precepts.
Free. Alive. Brave. Honest. Bold. Awake. Fierce.

Contents

I am quite young when I first learn that boys are better than girls because God made it so. No one says this to me quite so explicitly, but the grown-ups do tell me, when I ask (I am always asking about things), that God created men to be the head of the house, and God wants only men to be preachers. They try to tell me that this is perfectly fair and nothing to be upset about, but it is hard to lie to a child and get away with it because children are still intimately connected to their emotions. Children are able to feel things about God and about reality that grown-ups have forgotten how to feel.

Maybe as early as six, I sense that the setup isn't fair for girls. Surely God created us and loves us equal to boys. I feel it in my preindoctrinated bones that girls are, in fact, awesome.

Like most people, I eventually forget my early knowing. The gender dogma gets to me, gets inside me. I begin to believe it without really believing it and thus act in accordance with the inherited belief system but in contradiction to my innate wisdom. In other words, I grow up and begin to lose myself.

As a young reader, I find I am drawn to stories about tomboys—not because I am especially tomboyish myself but because tomboys are the closest approximation I have to a hero who looks like me. I notice that by rejecting what is girl-ish, the tomboys are sometimes allowed to do the cool things usually reserved for actual boys. I take this as prescriptive for my own life and begin to reject aspects of my femininity, not necessarily because I am more masculine by nature as some of us are, but because I have internalized that *girl* = something bad. The dogma has infiltrated my emotional self and my self-perception. Indoctrination has begun.

The religion in which I am raised teaches that we are all born "lost" and must be saved from our original sin. In reality, I am born in possession of my own soul, but as I grow, the world tries to take her from me. Not knowing any better, I let them, and ever so slowly, over time, my soul becomes lost. I am not born into lostness so much as I am led there by the insidious ploys of patriarchy before I am old enough to know I can resist.

But eventually, I discover the nearly invisible, totally insev-erable cord that links the self to the soul—my original goodness and beauty and essence, my *imago Dei*. Alas, she is not really lost. My soul is just in hiding from the onslaught of oppressive dogma. I can recover her.

This is *very* good news. I follow the cord all the way to reunion. What I have ultimately been saved from in this life is not my depravity; rather, I have been saved from the clutches of patriarchy that tried to sever me from myself.

This is my story. Her story. Our story.

CHAPTER 1

But God Is a Boy!

Two of my all-time favorite Bible characters are Eldad and Medad from Numbers 11. Totally cliché, I know (just kidding). In case you're unfamiliar with their story, it happened like this.

Moses gathered up seventy elders around the tent of meeting, and suddenly the Spirit fell upon them, and they all began to prophesy. But there was this one little hiccup. The seventy prophesying elders were at *the tent*—you know, the important place where God was supposed to show up. The tent, like a temple or a synagogue or a church, was exactly where everyone expected God to be.

But meanwhile, these two rogue prophets, Eldad and Medad, were still down at the camp with the people. They started prophesying too—not at the tent, with the seventy approved elders at the approved location, but at camp. Joshua, Moses's assistant, caught wind of this aberrant behavior, and it totally freaked him out. He ran to Moses in a panic and said, "My lord Moses, stop them!"

I mean, can you imagine something so horrible as unsupervised, unauthorized-by-Moses, out-among-the-ordinary-people prophesying? Moses's response to Joshua was epic.

Moses said, "Are you jealous for my sake? Would that all the Lord's people were prophets, and that the Lord would put his spirit on them!" And as calmly as that, he returned to camp with the seventy elders. The end.

The first time I preached about Eldad and Medad, it was Pentecost Sunday, and the great irony of it all was that during the service, a man stood up (dragging his family of women behind him) and walked out of church. He wrote me a letter to let me know that if only I would just study the Bible, I would know that I, a woman, was not authorized to preach to men. His name was Tom.

I call him Joshua for short.

For whatever reason, we humans are always trying to reinstate the limitations God has blown apart, as if God needs our help wrangling things back under control. We're always getting worked up and bothered on behalf of God, feeling threatened for Christ, reacting to change like a porcupine with an overactive startle reflex.

There's hardly a topic in the church today that brings out more quills than messing with gender, or, to state it more plainly, messing with patriarchy. One Sunday, our worship minister and I decided to sing "She's Got the Whole World in Her Hands" during a worship service. After church, I received an email that said, "If we cannot even sing '*He's* Got the Whole World in His Hands' without your interference of changing the gender of Almighty God to serve your own sick needs, then we have a problem with you. Your sick need to glorify females over males is a deal breaker and church destructor. You are sick and need help." The same man continued to harass me for months, though he left our male music minister alone. I think it's worth noting that in all my years of singing about God in exclusively male terms, I have never once received an angry email from a congregant complaining that the way we elevate men over women is sick and disgusting.

Another time, I called to check on a congregant I had not seen in a while. He'd left the congregation, he told me over the phone, because I was a man-hater. I tried to assure him that I did not hate men at all, but I was unable to persuade him. He had been listening to my sermons, and they were all the evidence he needed to prove that I was unequivocally antiman. He said—and I will never forget this—that I was poisoning the minds of little girls. His words stung. I liked this guy; I'd been in his home to visit his ill wife.

I HAD USED MY VOICE FROM THE PULPIT TO CHALLENGE GENDER NORMS, AND ONCE THOSE TRUTHS ARE SPOKEN AND BIRTHED, NO AMOUNT OF AFTER-THE-FACT GENDER-CONDITIONED BEHAVIOR CAN ERASE THEM POSTPARTUM.

Even though I knew he was mistaken, it did not feel good to be seen in such a light, to have my message of empowerment characterized as poison. In retrospect, I wish I had asked him, Have you ever challenged any of your male pastors when they spoke of a male God? Have you ever called them antiwoman? Did you demand that they stop poisoning the minds of little boys? But alas, women are expected to be silent in conflict, and due to centuries of conditioning, I held my tongue. Attempted to make him feel better. My tried-and-true "womanly" responses did not work, even though we met up for lunch after the phone call and I tried even harder. He never came back to my church, and I suspect it was because by the time I attempted to do the tender dance required of women who lead, it was too late. I had used my voice from the pulpit to challenge gender norms, and once those truths are spoken and birthed, no amount of after-the-fact, gender-conditioned behavior can erase them postpartum.

Frankly, this is good news. Out of habit, too often I find myself apologizing for what I've already spoken into being, but (thank God) those unneeded apologies never can quite erase what I've said. No matter how much a woman stutters and trips over her own becoming, a woman cannot unbecome. This is grace.

Once you begin to see just how unbalanced our language about God has been, you cannot unsee it. I cannot hear complaints about feminine language for God without remembering the countless times in my upbringing that I heard God referred to in exclusively male terms and the way that exclusivity damaged my psyche. As Mary Daly says, "If God is man, then man is God." And if woman is not good enough to be God, but man *is* good enough, then man is better than woman.

WHETHER WE IDENTIFY AS MALE OR FEMALE OR SOMEWHERE BETWEEN OR BEYOND THE BINARY, WE ARE EACH NEGATIVELY AFFECTED BY THE FALSE VALUE SYSTEM IN WHICH MALE = MORE DIVINE AND FEMALE = LESS.

In college, I heard a (rather poor) sermon on the necessity of Christ's maleness. The not-surprisingly-male preacher argued that the historic Jesus *had to* be a man, by which he meant "masculine"—that is, tough, strong, manly, able to bear the hardship of life as God-in-flesh. The unspoken implication, of course, was that a woman could not have borne such a spiritual weight. She was not strong enough; she was too weak to be God. The even deeper implication was that when the Scriptures proclaim God created male and female in the image of God, that is, in fact, a lie—or at least a distortion—because only a male could be the vessel of incarnation. For if men *and women* are equally image-bearers of the divine, then God could just as readily be revealed in woman as in man. But according to this preacher, Jesus had to be a man. Women are lesser vessels through whom God cannot work or reveal God's self in the same way.

Of course, almost all of us could name a holy or saintly woman in our lives, and so we know this premise is nonsense. And yet, even though we know it to be false experientially, this notion that women are somehow less capable of divine revelation and divine connection persists and poisons our view of self even today. Whether we identify as male or female or somewhere between or beyond the binary, we are each negatively affected by the false value system in which male = more divine and female = less.

I know that for me, the inherent less-ness of being female seeped into my consciousness from childhood. I still distinctly remember a conversation I had in high school in which a friend said confidently that a woman could never be president because women are "too emotional." This wasn't a line from the Bible, but it was accepted as gospel truth, plain as the nose on your face. For me, a rational, thinker type (INTJ on the Myers-Briggs) and also a woman, this accusation about *the* woman's temperament (as if we were all the same) didn't make sense. But one cannot point out logic in these situations without being accused of being emotional because, as a woman, to have an opinion is to have an emotion. At least, that is how our thoughts are so often handled—as nonthoughts, as feelings that we dressed up in words and trotted out like dolls at a tea party to be admired but certainly not taken seriously.

My partner, who happens to be transgender, is remarkably confident for a woman, and every time I marvel at her confidence, she grins and tells me that there are some benefits to having been raised as a boy. We are both women, but because she was perceived as a boy growing up and I was perceived as a girl, we have been socially conditioned in radically different ways. This is not to say cisgender women cannot be confident or be raised to be confident (and, I might add, many trans women have their confidence knocked flat by a cruel society after transition—my girlfriend happens to be one of the lucky ones who emerged still standing), but to be a woman *and* confident usually requires strong and persistent countercultural messaging, to which many women do not have enough access.

Men, on the other hand, are often treated as more-than from birth (God is man, so man is God), and this too wounds. In 2015, a man named Glen Dukes in San Antonio was convicted of forcing five women into prostitution and of tying one of them to a chair, suffocating her with a plastic bag, and setting her on fire. What disturbs me more than Glen Dukes's violent actions, however, is the approach his defense attorney—a man, who, I presume, has *not* set any women on fire and appears, by all accounts, to be an upstanding member of society—took during the trial. He said to the jury, "Glen Dukes, quite frankly, is a man who loves women. He wants relationships with women, but he doesn't want just one."

> **TO BE A WOMAN AND CONFIDENT USUALLY REQUIRES STRONG AND PERSISTENT COUNTERCULTURAL MESSAGING, TO WHICH MANY WOMEN DO NOT HAVE ENOUGH ACCESS.**

This presumably decent, law-abiding lawyer confused murder with love and thought it a perfectly acceptable form of defense to use with his coed jury in the twenty-first century, but his behavior is by no means an anomaly. A 2020 study by the UN Development Programme found that one-third of people (men *and women*) worldwide believe it is okay for a man to beat his wife. The absurd yet common acceptance of violence against women as a normal part of men's relationships with women tells us that something is terribly, terribly wrong with the way our world approaches gender.

Is it possible to fix the problem, and if so, where do we begin? As a theologian, I start with God. What we believe about who God is constitutes a huge part of the problem, but shifting the way we think about God can also be a significant part of the solution. When we think of the Christian story of the incarnation, we might ask why God didn't just appear in flesh as a woman so as to eliminate this false equation between God and maleness once and for all. Why not a Christa figure to usher in God's queendom rather than kingdom? Like, if Christ had simply shown up with breasts, would that have been enough to scandalize the patriarchy into retreat?

In recent history, various feminist theologians and artists have imagined Christ in female form—perhaps most strikingly, a female Christ on the cross. The first female Christ on a cross, named *Christa*, was a 250-pound statue created by Edwina Sandys in 1974. Its first appearance in a cathedral in 1984 was short lived after the cathedral received many angry letters, and the bishop at the time ordered *Christa* to be taken down, calling it "theologically and historically indefensible." He said it was "desecrating our symbols." But from my perspective, *Christa* elevated the symbol of the cross by helping make it more universally accessible to all.

Since then, other artists have created their own versions of a female Christ, and to me, each one is as haunting as the next. The first time I saw a female crucifix depicted in art, I thought immediately of battered and abused women. More pointedly, I saw myself. As a survivor of sexual assault and domestic abuse, when I saw the feminine form on the cross, I suddenly saw the Christ as someone who entered my suffering with me, and the cross took on a whole new meaning for me. This imaginative yet deeply theological art has the power to speak directly to a woman's experience. Not only do we see God depicted in art *as woman*; we see *our female suffering*—the battering of bodies and suppression of our souls—displayed in the crucifixion, which hints at Christ's solidarity with our suffering and our claim to resurrection. In these depictions, Christ is not the "head" over us so much as the human body beside us, beaten as we are, despised as we are, yet capable of rising—in fact, destined by God's own design to rise.

As powerful as a female image of Christ is, I don't want to lose the male images of Christ either. After all, a male version of God who willingly divests himself of power is far more revolutionary than a woman who is murdered by those in power. Women are crucified on the daily. Men with power are not.

> **CHRIST IS NOT THE "HEAD" OVER US SO MUCH AS THE HUMAN BODY BESIDE US, BEATEN AS WE ARE, DESPISED AS WE ARE, YET CAPABLE OF RISING.**

The kenosis of Christ—that is, the self-emptying act of God—is more earth shattering precisely because it happened in male form. When I was completing my training as a spiritual director, one of our male lecturers spoke in a way that was very triggering to several women in the room who had experienced abuse. His intentions were good, but he was clueless about the impact of his words and manner of speaking. I kept quiet throughout the lecture even though my insides were in tumult, and afterward, I processed quietly with a few other women. The leaders of the training—both men—caught wind of the way women in the group had been triggered, and to my astonishment and amazement, in collaboration with some of the women, they created a safe container the following day for people to express their feelings and be heard with honor and care. I rarely ever cry in public, but I found myself weeping because over and over again in my ministry, I create safe containers for others in the aftermath of abusive or triggering situations. Never had someone created the container for me in a communal setting—and certainly I had never seen such swift listening or such sensitive follow-up crafted humbly and willingly by those with power. Generally speaking, men do not give their power away for free or even share it nicely.

THE CRUCIFIXION OF WOMEN, I AM ALREADY FAMILIAR WITH. THAT STORY IS VERY OLD, AND I KNOW IT IN MY BONES AND MY LINEAGE. THE STORY OF WOMAN RISING—THAT IS THE NARRATIVE MY WOUNDED SOUL MOST NEEDS.

That the Christ had power *equal to God* but did not consider it something to be exploited but rather emptied himself, taking the form of a servant, is remarkably countercultural to the patriarchy. If Christ as a *woman* had done the same thing, she would simply have been doing what had been expected of her all along—that she lay down her life for everyone else. When I think about the scene of the crucifixion, I find a male image of Christ compelling because only the willing death of a male-presenting God could topple the power structures of the time. The death of a female-presenting God would scarcely have raised an eyebrow.

It is at the scene of the resurrection that I most crave a Christa. The crucifixion of women, I am already familiar with.

That story is very old, and I know it in my bones and my lineage. The story of woman rising—that is the narrative my wounded soul most needs. As in Maya Angelou's poem "And Still I Rise," women who resurrect are an inspiring force:

> Did you want to see me broken?
> Bowed head and lowered eyes?
> Shoulders falling down like teardrops,
> Weakened by my soulful cries?
>
> You may shoot me with your words,
> You may cut me with your eyes,
> You may kill me with your hatefulness,
> But still, like air, I'll rise.

If I could retell the Christ story in my own words, he would die as a man and be raised as a woman. Such creative license is not so far-fetched. Women, after all, play pivotal roles in the historical accounts of the resurrection: it is always the women who see and experience and tell about the resurrection *first*. The resurrection, it seems to me, is decidedly feminine in the biblical account. This is not to say men are not present, but in a reversal of many religious stories, the men come along behind, receiving what the women know and experience rather than telling the women what to know and experience. Can you see how different this is from the passive femininity we've come to expect in women? Naturally, the men first try to tell the women that they are mistaken (perhaps the women have made it all up in their heads, like women are so prone to do). Depending on your translation, the women's words are called an "idle tale," "nonsense," or even "insanity," which is so very familiar to us women who have tried to tell the truth about things but found our words dismissed. But in this case, alleluia, the men are wrong and willing (eventually) to admit it.

Unlike the patriarchal powers that try to dominate and control religious experience, the women at the resurrection simply bear witness to what they have seen, and others are invited to come and see for themselves, to join if they so choose. The women make religious experience invitational rather than mandatory, and the invitation is to life, not death. Can you see how different this spirituality is from the kind of religion that demands ideological agreement? Through the power of invitation and sharing, the spiritual experience is made accessible to all.

Christ shares power rather than lording it over others. This sharing got him in trouble with the other lords, but ultimately it gained him the final victory—life over death. Can you see how different this is from the toxic masculinity we have come to accept? Christ's actions counter the "masculinity" that prizes the hoarding of power rather than the sharing of it, and it is precisely this giving away of power that leads Christ into the power of the resurrection.

All of this makes me wonder whether the resurrected Christ's "reign" should be best understood as a queendom rather than a kingdom. Are our notions of kingdom too tainted by hierarchy and patriarchy to be useful in understanding this upside-down reality of the Christ?

I am certainly not the first to question the usage of *kingdom*; it is, after all, merely an imperfect translation of the Greek word *basileia*, so there is nothing particularly sacred about the English word. Dr. Ada Maria Isasi-Diaz, mother of *mujerista* theology, popularized the term *kindom* as an alternative—as in, "we are all kin to one another." I like kindom. In a kindom, no one is dependent on the oppression of anyone else. We can imagine Christ's "reign" as one world family united by love.

In this book I choose to use the word *queendom* for its sheer power to shock and disrupt. I think *kingdom* is too contaminated by patriarchy to be effective. I think of how the misogynistic preacher Mark Driscoll once described Jesus as a "prize-fighter with a tattoo down His leg, a sword in His hand and the commitment to make someone bleed." While most Christians would denounce Driscoll's violent portrayal of Christ, our notions of a kingdom are still influenced by characteristics of domination, coercion, and unchecked power. I believe the misuse of *kingdom* has so damaged our bodies, our religion, and our psyches that we need to be shocked out of our complacency. We need a word Driscoll would never entertain. We need a word that agitates the Joshuas and stokes the fires of our imaginations.

By using *queendom*, I am not suggesting a mere hierarchal swap whereby women are now on high and men grovel down below. Such a vision would be far too shortsighted. Rather, the use of a gendered word encourages us to think of Christ's "reign" as something brand new rather than an improved replica of the old systems. Christ is *not* Monarchy 2.0 (like the old kings, only better); Christ is the opposite of the old way. But what is the opposite of a kingdom? Anarchy, perhaps, like what we find at the end of the book of Judges. *Or*, the opposite of a kingdom can be imagined as a queendom, in which the old values are reversed, the oppressive structures are toppled, and the sharing of power is equitable and expected. Can I get an amen?

> I BELIEVE THE MISUSE OF KINGDOM *HAS SO DAMAGED OUR BODIES, OUR RELIGION, AND OUR PSYCHES THAT WE NEED TO BE SHOCKED OUT OF OUR COMPLACENCY.*

I think it is worth noting here that archeological evidence suggests the matrilineal, goddess-worshipping societies of the ancient Neolithic period were more egalitarian than the patriarchal ones that followed. Thus by proposing something "brand new," we may in fact be returning to something that is very, very ancient. To use familiar theological language, patriarchy can be understood as a distortion, a fallen-ness, and a turning away from what God originally intended. Patriarchy is a sin from which Christ seeks to redeem and restore the earth. Christ ushers us into a queendom where God moves not with dominion but with love.

I use *queendom* not because I want to elevate women over men but because I want to level the playing field. *Kingdom* has been overused and misunderstood for far too long. I do not think we can balance the theological scales by adding a drop or two of nonbinary language about God. We need a heavy word, a weighted word, a word with some authority. *Queendom of God* implies strongly that women are just as capable of bearing the divine image as we have always believed men are. *Queendom* makes us rethink our preconceptions. *Queendom* allows us to imagine that God-in-Christ really is disrupting the world and making all things new.

THE OPPOSITE OF A KINGDOM CAN BE IMAGINED AS A QUEENDOM, IN WHICH THE OLD VALUES ARE REVERSED, THE OPPRESSIVE STRUCTURES ARE TOPPLED, AND THE SHARING OF POWER IS EQUITABLE AND EXPECTED.

In the progressive Baptist congregation I pastored in Waco, it was not uncommon for us to use feminine pronouns for God. Most of the time we avoided gendering God at all, but when we did, we tried to sprinkle some feminine language in and around the traditional masculine imagery of God. Women would tell me how moving it was for them not only to see two female ministers breaking bread and presiding over communion but also to hear God spoken of as Mother, as Feminine Spirit, as She. Still, we used it sparingly. We believed God was neither male nor female but beyond gender altogether, so we didn't simply want to swap out one dangerously idolatrous image of God for another. We were aware that all images of God ultimately fall short. To adhere too closely to any of them would be to our own detriment.

I USE QUEENDOM *PRECISELY FOR ITS TOO-MUCH-NESS, BECAUSE WHY SHOULD* QUEEN *BE TOO MUCH, TOO FAR, WHEN* KING *IS NOT?*

Then one year I was out of town, and my youth minister preached in my place. Since it was Pentecost, the day of the church year so closely associated with the Holy Spirit, and since *spirit* is a feminine word in Hebrew, he chose to preach his sermon using exclusively feminine pronouns for God. The liturgy throughout the service reflected the same exclusivity—all Shes, no Hes. That was the Sunday we discovered the limits of this progressive community. God as a She every now and then, like a little wild card to keep you awake and make you think, was tolerable. What was not tolerable for some members of our congregation was a She who took up *all* the space one Sunday out of thousands. It didn't even matter that She was being spoken of by a man. She, on her own, without the balance of male pronouns, was just *too much.*

I use *queendom* precisely for its too-much-ness, because why should *queen* be too much, too far, when *king* is not? The fact that this word makes people bristle is proof that we have a serious problem. I use *queendom* because of its power to disrupt, to shake us up, to rattle us loose. I use *queendom* for its power.

I keep circling back in my mind to Glen Dukes and his defense attorney because those sorts of explanations of violence against women have become so commonplace for us. The notion persists in our culture that the exploitation of women is due to the male sex drive rather than a male impotence to be humane and an impotence to be tender.

The Latin origins of the word *impotence* are connected to violence and fury, and I would suggest that men do not dominate and violate when they are strong. They dominate when they are frail. No man ever silences a woman in service of God. A man only silences a woman in service of his own insecurity.

Anybody can see that Glen Dukes doesn't love women. He hates them. And if you dug deeper than that, you'd find he hates his own weakness. A sexual drive isn't the problem. Sex can be intimate, and sex can be good. The problem is impotence—the inability to be vulnerable, to be intimate, to be loving. It is cowardice that craves control over closeness.

NO MAN EVER SILENCES A WOMAN IN SERVICE OF GOD. A MAN ONLY SILENCES A WOMAN IN SERVICE OF HIS OWN INSECURITY.

When religious leaders continue to silence women, it is a sign of the church's impotence, not its fidelity.

But from what I've seen, no matter how many Joshuas try to beat them into silence, the women I know keep resurrecting, along with their voices, as if equality were a force that cannot be killed.

Women are potent. Women are fertile. Women are strong. Which is why we don't need more violence. Why we don't need more kingdoms. Would that all people be filled with power, *even* the men, may it be so, amen.

THY QUEENDOM COME

Our Mother, who art in heaven,
Hallowed be thy name,
Thy Queendom come,
Thy love be revealed,
On earth as it is in heaven.
Give us this day our daily bread.
Forgive us the proclivity to exert power over,
Liberate us with power from within.
And lead us not into temptation,
But deliver us from evil,
For this is your Queendom,
Where power and glory are shared. Amen.

CHAPTER 2

The Reign of Love

Judges 19 tells a story of a Levite and his concubine. Levites, you may remember, were supposed to be special men, set apart for God. She, on the other hand, was less than even the wife of a Levite—she was secondary, added later, whether for children or for pleasure or for both. Surprisingly, she had left him (that didn't happen too much in those days), but he went after her to fetch her back. As they were traveling home, an old man took them in to feed them and give them a night's stay.

From there, the story quickly becomes grotesque. While they were relaxing in the old man's home, men of the city surrounded the house, pounded on the door, and demanded that the host send out the Levite and let them gang-rape him.

But the old man pled with them, "No! Please don't commit such an evil act, given that this man has come to my home as a guest. Don't do this vile thing." Then he tried to make them another offer instead: "Here is my virgin daughter and the Levite's concubine. Let me send them out, and you can abuse them and do whatever you want to them." More literally, what he says is this: "Ravish them, and do to them the good in your eyes."

Notice here the contrast in his speech. What the men wanted to do to his male guest? He called it vile. When he offered the two women, he invited the men to ravish them, saying, "Do what is good in your eyes." Evil. Good. Same act. Different victims.

Despite his attempts to distract them, the men of the city did not listen. The Levite saw that the words and promises weren't working and did the only thing he could think of doing that might distract them from their target: he gave them a body, a human body. He shoved his concubine outside and slammed the door behind her before anyone could get a foothold inside. His plan worked. The evil men left him alone. He was safe.

The same could not be said for her. She was raped and abused until daybreak, when they finally released her. She returned to the old man's house and collapsed at the door-step, her hands gripping the threshold, as if she'd been trying to hold on for dear life. When her husband found her there in the morning, she didn't speak or move. It's unclear in the text whether she was dead or paralyzed from trauma and pain, but either way, she didn't move. So he picked her up and carried her home, and upon arriving home, just as you'd expect, he got to work chopping her body into twelve separate pieces.

He shipped her parts out to the twelve tribes of Israel to make a point. He wanted them to know what had been done to him (*him*, not *her*!).

If you can believe it, from here, things got even worse. The tribes were outraged by the news. They went to war against the Benjamites, the tribe from whom the rapists came, and tens of thousands of soldiers were slain on both sides. Eventually, Israel won out against the Benjamites, and they massacred the city—all the women, children, even animals. Only six hundred men escaped. It got worse. After the war was over, the Israel-ites started to feel bad because the remaining Benjamites were left without wives and no way to procreate. To remedy this predicament, they slaughtered all the people in Jabesh-Gilead except for the virgins, and then they gave the remaining four hundred virgins to the lonely Benjamites. It got worse. There were only four hundred virgins but six hundred Benjamite men, so if you do the math, they needed two hundred more. So next they abducted two hundred women from Shiloh. In other words, the rape of one quickly escalated into the rape of six hundred, not to mention the slaughter of thousands more. And this is how the book of Judges ends. No redemption. No reconciliation. No resurrection.

Arguably, this is one of the worst stories, if not the worst story, in the whole Bible, and you might wonder why the biblical writers would choose to include something so graphic in a sacred text. It's no wonder it didn't make an appearance in our Sunday school curriculum as children. But the biblical writers had a plan. Like any good storytellers, they wanted to make sure we would be ready for the next scene: the establishment of the Israelite monarchy in 1 Samuel. I have many things to say about this story, but for now, let it suffice to say that we are meant to leave the book of Judges longing for a king who can set things right.

Enter the hero of the Israelite story, King David. King David, champion over Goliath. King David, a man after God's own heart. King David, who appears in the lineage of Christ.

But if you read King David's story through the eyes of women, he is far less impressive. Bathsheba, who is far too often mischaracterized as a loose woman, was merely minding her own business when David summoned her to his quarters to sleep with her. It is safe to assume, based on the power dynamics between a king and a common woman, that the encounter was not consensual. And when this encounter got her pregnant?

David's solution was to kill Bathsheba's husband to cover it all up. I wrote the following poem, "Another Woman," about David's history with women:

> i'm not saying it wasn't awful
> for Bathsheba
> to marry the man
> who raped her then
> murdered her lover
> still, at least she has a name
> a story
> a son
> i am just one more woman
> from David's harem
> you don't know anything about me

To make matters worse, two short chapters after Bathsheba's story, David's own daughter, Tamar, was raped by her half-brother, David's son, Amnon. In response, David did nothing.

If you're paying attention to the women in the story, the monarchy was no better than the anarchy at the end of Judges. The monarchy did not help women. It did not help the lowly or the marginalized. The kings did not help. The kings were disasters. Could we all just agree the answer doesn't lie with kings?

So what then? A queen?

• • • • •

Today as I write this, it is Good Friday, that day full of death we defiantly call good. All around me today people are dying—the usual deaths and the unusual pandemic deaths. It is 2020, the year of the COVID-19 pandemic, and it is a frightening time to be alive. But today I hear the birds singing, chirping their joy, oblivious to our plight.

When Jesus breathed his last, were all the birds so blissfully unaware as they are today?

On Good Friday, I always think of Leila, my daughter. I didn't give birth to her physically, but I labored so hard to become her mother. When I first met her in the NICU, where she had spent six lonely weeks without any family, I was overwhelmed with all-encompassing love. The caseworker, the social worker, and the nurses thought for sure this abandoned infant needed adopting and that God had sent me in her lonely hour to be a mother. I felt it too—the supernatural, larger-than-life bond; the drive to protect; the consuming desire to nurture and care. She was, without doubt, the best gift I had ever been given. I vowed to hold her gently always.

THE MONARCHY DID NOT HELP WOMEN. IT DID NOT HELP THE LOWLY OR THE MARGINALIZED. THE KINGS DID NOT HELP.

I loved, loved, loved being her mother, but five weeks into our bonding, a previously unknown family member came forward who wanted her. Though I had been her only mother all those weeks, they had a biological tie, and I did not.

The judge said my baby girl would be leaving for good on Good Friday, 2018. I don't remember the birds outside the courthouse that day, but surely they were there, singing their sweet release while I stumbled toward my car, sick with grief. My baby was leaving.

Of course, when you become a foster parent, you are entering into a delicate and complicated system. You know the children are not "yours," though you pledge to love them fully and without reservation. You know your care may very well be temporary and that a happy, safe reunification with family would be a good thing. (I still have an ongoing and positive relationship with the biological mother of another baby I had the privilege of fostering.) And yet, in Leila's case, after some unsettling interactions with her new caretakers, I felt apprehensive. Something didn't seem right, and I couldn't shake the feeling that Leila might not be okay. But the courts do not ask foster parents for an opinion. You are the silent provider, giving all your love to a vulnerable child with no means to protect them from future harm. And so on Good Friday 2018, I said goodbye to my baby, unable to stop the tears as the caseworker loaded her tiny, fragile body into an infant car seat, carried her out, and drove away.

I left that same day for retreat. I couldn't bear to stay home, surrounded by the emptiness of her absence. I could not stick around to preach an Easter sermon to my congregation from my grief-stricken body. And so I visited some wilderness space near the sea—one of my familiar, go-to retreat spots—and there I walked the grounds and felt my sadness for three days. I kept

IN A QUEENDOM RULED BY LOVE, THERE IS NO SUCH THING AS DOMINATION. CONTROL IS EXPOSED FOR THE ILLUSION THAT IT IS.

thinking of the women who stayed by Jesus all the way to the bitter end and then beyond, visiting his tomb with spices, refusing to abandon their love. I thought most of Mary, his mother—how she had labored to give him birth and, before that, labored to say yes to his arrival in her womb. How she had labored to love him all his life without holding on too tightly. How Good Friday was undoubtedly the worst day of her life. How she had to let him go. How she could not protect him despite being his mother.

My own story, like Mary's, did not end on Good Friday, which I will share with you later, but the point right now is to say that the queendom of God looks like mother-love and nothing like a regime. In a queendom ruled by love, there is no such thing as domination. Control is exposed for the illusion that it is. We are wrapped in the kind of mother-love for humanity and creation that never clings too tightly, does not coerce or force, does not hoard or possess but loves freely and with abandon.

Mary allowed Jesus to fulfill his destiny, even though it caused her and him great pain and suffering. She did not try to keep him safe. She set him free to be good, brave, and fully alive. She relinquished control of his choices and his future, and before he even entered this world, she relinquished control of what people would think of *her*, an unwed mother. She set *herself* free to be good, brave, and fully alive.

My own journey as a foster mom has taught me so much about nonpossessive love. People often say to me that they couldn't do what I do, meaning they could not welcome a child into their home knowing they might have to say goodbye someday. People mean well when they say this, as if they are expressing their admiration. But what I want to say back is, Do you think this is easier for me than it would be for you? Do you think I possess some special ability that you do not with which I can magically fall deeply in love with a beautiful child and then let go of them without feeling excruciating pain? I have been granted no such ability. My love is fierce, and that means I ache with agony at every goodbye. And honestly, I believe only people capable of feeling profound pain and loss should be foster parents because if your love isn't deep and full, then you aren't giving these children what they most need to heal from their trauma. The kind of love fostering requires is not so different from the kind of love all good parenting and partnering requires—a love that does not cling too tight, a love that can let go when needed.

It's not enough to say that the queendom of God is ruled by love if we do not define what kind of love we mean. We've too often been misled into equating love with clinging, with possession, and with ownership. "You belong to me," we say about people we love. "You're my person. Be mine." We try to manipulate relationships so people will stay with us, we sabotage each other's growth so we don't get left behind, we try to control who our children become. I remember the day I locked myself in the bathroom to escape my then husband's screaming and abuse. He slid a copy of our wedding vows under the bathroom door as a way to tell me that I had no way out because I had promised to stay in the name of love. "Love" becomes a prison when it is a force for control rather than an offering, a gift.

IN THE QUEENDOM OF GOD, LOVE IS A LIBERATING FORCE, A PERMISSION-GRANTING FORCE, AN EMPOWERING ENERGY THAT EXPANDS YOU, NEVER SHRINKS YOU.

In the queendom of God, love is a liberating force, a permission-granting force, an empowering energy that expands you, never shrinks you. Rather than viewing the other as an "object" of love, in the queendom, we view one another as full participants in a relationship with the freedom to make our own choices.

Another way to say this is that the queendom of God has no queen because love is no aristocracy, no monocracy. We're not merely replacing a powerful king with a powerful queen. This is not a reversal of the hierarchy; it is the obliteration of hierarchy.

When Mary was still with child, she sang a song known as the Magnificat, part of which goes like this:

God has brought down rulers from their thrones
but has lifted up the humble.
God has filled the hungry with good things
but has sent the rich away empty.

It would be too easy to make this song about a simple swap—the proud are brought low, and the humble now rule. But we know that power can corrupt even those who start out with none. I think what Mary imagines is like the prophet Isaiah's leveling vision, in which "every valley shall be raised up, every mountain and hill be made low"—a statement that is quoted by the author of Luke just a few short chapters after Mary's song appears. Mary envisioned, conceived, and gave birth to a Holy Leveling. Think about it: Jesus didn't organize a coup, replacing himself as the new dictator, a kinder version than the ones before him. Jesus set to work on a spiritual plane, and he spent his time among the lowly and downtrodden—not to make kings of them but to restore their humanity. And when he drove the money changers out of the temple or called the Pharisees a "brood of vipers," I think his motivation was, in fact, similar. He wanted to restore to the corrupted powers their humanity, their souls.

THIS IS NOT A REVERSAL OF THE HIERARCHY; IT IS THE OBLITERATION OF HIERARCHY.

When I suggest a leveling rather than a reversal, this is not to soften Mary's song. Losing *any* power feels threatening to the privileged, and Mary's song is very, very threatening. In India, the East India Company forbade its recitation during evening prayer, lest the idea of "putting down the mighty from their seat" be taken too literally. In the 1980s, Guatemala also forbade the Magnificat from being recited publicly because its message was too revolutionary. In Argentina, mothers took up Mary's Magnificat as their cry when their children were abducted during the Dirty War. The women gathered together for a vigil, and they sang Mary's words for their lost children. They printed Mary's words on posters and hung them on street corners and in windows until, in 1977, the government of Argentina outlawed any public display of the lyrics. A Holy Leveling is a threat to those with power because it means losing power over others.

MARY'S VISION IS RADICAL AND UNSETTLING, AND IF YOU BENEFIT IN ANY WAY FROM THE PATRIARCHY, MARY OUGHT TO MAKE YOU UNCOMFORTABLE WHEN SHE SINGS.

When talking about a Holy Leveling, I recognize that in reality, your congregation may need a pastor, your committee may need a chair, your organization may need a president. I'm not suggesting that there is no need for leadership or structure or that we should return to the "good ole days" of anarchy like at the end of Judges, but I do believe that in the queendom of God, leadership is approached collaboratively and with a nonhierarchal bent. Queendom citizens work to ensure that all voices, from the "greatest" to the "least," can be heard, and the very categories of greatest and least are challenged on an ongoing basis. Leaders are the ones who ensure that deep and equitable listening happens without toxic interference. No one gets more of a voice just because they give more money or because they are older, or are younger, or have been there longer, or are related to someone important, or are white and male and cisgender. In the queendom, we elevate and center those voices that have been on the margins for far too long.

The powers will try to convince you that this centering of other voices is the suppression of *their* voices, but this is not so. It might *feel like* suppression to them because they are used to having the floor all the time. But the only way "leveling" works is if those who have been doing all the talking learn when to be quiet, when to yield the floor, and when to ask questions rather than assert answers. Mary's vision is radical and unsettling, and if you benefit in any way from the patriarchy, Mary ought to make you uncomfortable when she sings.

For all these reasons and more, I love the Mother Mary. If we allow it, she consistently upsets our normal understanding of things. She challenges our accepted norms about who is on top and whom it is that God blesses. She confronts in us the possessiveness of our own expressions of love with the open-armed way she loved her son. The veneration of her sainthood by the common people throughout the ages has kept the divine feminine alive amid a patriarchal institution's ambition to shut her out.

She even has the potential to flip our understanding of salvation itself. Our usual way of reading the biblical story views the Hebrew Scriptures as a setup for the coming of the Christ, savior of the world. Yet this savior narrative can be a detriment to women who are repetitively told not only that they are bad but also that they need someone outside themselves to save them. As women, we are the perpetual damsels in distress, only we have locked ourselves in our own towers due to our numerous "sins," and there is no hope of rescue except in the form of a male Christ who can forgive us and wipe our sins away while we wash his feet with our hair, sorrow, and tears.

The way I was raised to understand things, we women were sinners who could not trust ourselves a lick. After all, the "heart is deceitful above all things, and desperately wicked," which is an actual Bible verse I was required to memorize as a young child. I was conditioned to fear and mistrust my own self from the beginning.

Men were sinners too in this theological framework, but they had a closer connection with God and could still be preachers and leaders and such. Their sin was somehow not nearly as permanently damaging as the women's sin. I suppose this was because a woman ate the "apple" first, then practically forced it upon Adam. (Not the actual story, though it gets told like that.)

Even so, male or female, we all needed saving from the apple of original sin. We had no say in this; Eve had chosen for all of us, and we were doomed. I never liked this story, even as a child. It all seemed horribly unfair that none of us had any choice but were simply born bad because of one bad choice made thousands of years ago (six thousand years, to be exact, according to the creationists). But whether we liked it or not, we were stuck, and God, who was so good that he couldn't help but damn us all to eternal suffering for our sin, would eventually, after thousands more years, figure out a way to save relatively few of us while the rest of us plummeted onward to hell. And this we called the good news.

It was a horrible story. It didn't sit well with me, but just like my sin, I was stuck with it. This was my story.

But there is more than one way to read the Bible, to tell this story, and to understand faith. In fact, Christians have been telling the story in a whole variety of ways for their entire history, and not every version starts with how terrible we are and how vindictive God's righteousness required God to be. Whole other ways of talking about God and creation are available to us—ways that start with the image of God in every person, ways in which God's righteousness looks like love rather than violence and damnation. And those are just variations within the Christian story! Cultures across the ages have all sorts of ways of talking about God, and many of them do not ask me to believe in a God who would damn people to hell, then murder his son, all in the name of love. In other words, we don't have to accept that God was abusive and his abuse was the greatest form of love in the universe. We also need not tell the story in such a way that women bear the blame for sin and carry none of the gift of redemption.

What if we viewed the advent of God's kingdom not exclusively through the lens of Christ but also through Mary, the God-bearer? Thus a woman's salvation comes not from outside her but literally from within—from within her womb, the center of creativity, the place of her deep wisdom. This changes not just the way we view ourselves but how we live as spiritual beings. We are no longer waiting on a rescuer. We realize we are ready to conceive and give birth to new life in the virgin sense—a creative act between God and us, no masculine authority necessary. We can, as women, say yes to the divine annunciation, quite apart from any sinner's prayer, the blessing of priests, or deliverance by kings.

In 1851, Sojourner Truth, a woman born into slavery, delivered her famous speech "Ain't I a Woman?" to the Women's Rights Convention in Akron, Ohio. She said, "That little man in black there, he says women can't

> **THUS A WOMAN'S SALVATION COMES NOT FROM OUTSIDE HER BUT LITERALLY FROM WITHIN—FROM WITHIN HER WOMB, THE CENTER OF CREATIVITY, THE PLACE OF HER DEEP WISDOM.**

have as much rights as men, 'cause Christ wasn't a woman! Where did your Christ come from? Where did your Christ come from? From God and a woman! Man had nothing to do with him." She then uses the fact that the fall of humanity was blamed on Eve to women's advantage: "If the first woman God ever made was strong enough to turn the world upside down all alone, these women together ought to be able to turn it back and get it right side up again! And now they is asking to do it, the men better let them."

Such a view of salvation, in which a woman is in on the creative act, is empowering rather than disempowering. Instead of being utterly dependent on a savior, we are, like Mary, invited to give birth to God's saving work in our very own bodies. We are participants, not helpless prey trapped in sin's clutches, waiting for aid. We are empowered to come alongside the divine, working not for our salvation but *with* our salvation. Instead of believing we are worthy of death, we see ourselves through God's eyes and know that we are worthy of life.

Empowerment, though, is not the same as raw power. It is different than being in control. Being a mother taught me that. I was empowered to love fully and completely, but loving gave me no real dominion over life's affairs. There is so, so, so little that love can control, especially in other people. Perhaps this lack of dominion is true even for God. If loving meant controlling, you would expect God to prevent far more evil. But if loving includes allowing, then God's deep love means God will not restrict us, even when our choices are harmful. The mother-love of God looks nothing like control. It looks like unwavering faithfulness, abundance, provision, mercy.

> **WE ARE, LIKE MARY, INVITED TO GIVE BIRTH TO GOD'S SAVING WORK IN OUR VERY OWN BODIES.**

I had been fostering a new baby for several months after Leila left when I got a phone call from the caseworker asking if I could take a second baby into my home. I told her no because while I *wanted* to take care of all the babies, I was a single mom with a full-time pastorate, and I just didn't think I could take on another infant. But after we hung up, I had a nagging feeling. I called her back.

"You weren't asking about Leila, were you?" I asked.

"Yes. Leila has a broken femur, and we need to move her to another placement right away."

Why didn't you say so?! I thought. But I didn't say that. I just said, "Yes! Absolutely I will take her. I will take her. Please, let me take her."

So I ended up with two babies, by myself, both under the age of one, and one of them with a broken leg. I can't remember how, but somehow we all survived. Don't ask me when they got their first teeth or which one hit which milestone when because it's all a blur, but I can tell you all the teeth came—I even remembered to brush them (mostly)—and all the milestones were hit (eventually). My life was completely overcome with love. Love . . . and diapers. Two babies make five times more dirty diapers than one baby, I swear. But in and among the poop and spit-up and sleepless nights, there was double the love, double the joy, double the sweetness—which is not to say that love was easy or that I had any more control than I had the first time Leila came to me. After being in my home a full year, my second foster baby left my care, and after Leila had been with me for well over a year, I still couldn't adopt her. Her case had twists and turns, and even after things were looking good, there was one delay after another. I just wanted this kid to *be mine* already. But over and over again, I was reminded that motherhood is not ownership and that even after adoption day, control would forever be an illusion that would not serve me well.

THE MOTHER-LOVE OF GOD LOOKS NOTHING LIKE CONTROL. IT LOOKS LIKE UNWAVERING FAITHFULNESS, ABUNDANCE, PROVISION, MERCY.

When her adoption was finally scheduled, it was set for Ash Wednesday 2020, which struck me as so bizarre. After losing her on Good Friday, Easter would have seemed so much more appropriate. Pretty much any day of the year would have suited me just fine. But Ash Wednesday? The day Christians put ashes on our foreheads and reflect on how we will all die someday? I took this to be God's reminder that even now, I shouldn't hold on too tight.

And so when I adopted my daughter on Ash Wednesday, I thought of the Mother Mary and how motherhood is an exercise in letting go when your instincts scream at you to hold on. I woke early on adoption day, reflecting on how two years earlier, I had spent my Easter morning in a cemetery, sitting among gravestones because I felt like death and because that is what the women did—they went to his tomb early in the morning while it was still dark. In my own predawn grief that year, I could not imagine resurrection for me because my baby wasn't coming back, but around dawn, I did notice the sheet of wildflowers covering the graveyard. I remember the cemetery was so vivid with color, it was one of the most beautiful places I have ever been. Unexpectedly, I felt gratitude rise up in me, sprouting amid my grief without overshadowing it. Gratitude because I had received the incredible gift of loving this child completely and thoroughly, and love like that has healing in its wings, even as it flies away. I remember thinking that to have known her even for so brief a time was one of my life's greatest delights. Plopped among the headstones of unfamiliar names, I smiled for this child I had known in all her particularity.

I wasn't sure what to make of the fact that two years later, I was adopting her not on Easter but on Ash Wednesday, the day Christians remember our own frailty and the impermanency of life itself. This would be the day my daughter became "mine forever," the day I could relax because I wouldn't have to lose her again . . . but I will, in fact, lose her—over and over in a hundred ways, big and small, because motherhood is an exercise in letting go, and so I prayed that one Good Friday was enough to make a real mother out of me. That my grip would never inadvertently tighten around her neck the way love sometimes chokes in its effort to protect and preserve, the way love ceases to be love when grasping instead of holding. I wanted—I still want—to cling to my daughter. I never, ever want to lose her, except I know the very act of clinging could destroy her. And so I marked the forehead of this love with ashes, reminded myself from dust we came and to dust we shall return, and once again I practiced letting go, and in so doing, I kept the love alive for one more fragile-as-a-wildflower day.

There is no hierarchy among the wildflowers, which is as it should be. Consider the lilies of the field, my friend—their beauty as well as their impermanence. Their lack of competition. Their stunning diversity. Let's imagine a world with fewer thrones, more fields.

CHAPTER 3

It's an Inside Job First

I have a natural bent toward a contemplative life. I like silence. I like solitude. I like sitting still. When I discovered the rich tradition of Christian contemplative practices in my early twenties, I felt right at home. I had always communed with God in silence, in nature, and in the secret regions of the heart. Since childhood, I have been introspective and at times attuned to the quiet nudges of the Holy Spirit. What I didn't know was that contemplative Christians and mystics of all kinds had been encountering God in these sorts of quiet and unassuming ways for a very long time.

I spent years finding my own way before anyone taught me much about contemplative prayer. I found the most help in those early years from the biblical stories of the Israelites wandering the wilderness in search of the Promised Land. I resonated with them—traveling along unfamiliar territory, struggling with doubt, sometimes experiencing God's provision but other times wondering if God was paying attention at all. I felt a deep connection to the idea of manna, that small but tangible sign that God was with them, which they could not hoard for later. Manna taught me early on that I had to show up expectant every single day, give thanks for daily bread without clinging too tightly to the day's provision, and then begin again the next morning. If I kept my attention on the present, on the day-to-day, God would not disappoint. If I looked for big miracles or answers too soon, I would start to think that God had abandoned me. In short, I learned to be a wilderness traveler, which, though difficult, has served me well. My best friend from high school, Sara, journeyed with me, and if it had not been for one other fellow traveler, I might not have kept going, but because of her, I did.

Discovering the tradition of contemplative practices during seminary made me feel like I had been walking with hordes of other travelers throughout space and time. I just hadn't known about them. I had thought I was mostly alone, but it turned out I was very much in good company. Over the next several years, I began to spend more time with my fellow wanderers. I went on silent retreats, traveled to monasteries, joined a contemplative reading group that was slowly digesting the writings of mystics such as Thomas Merton, participated in liturgical prayers, walked labyrinths, learned the art of meditation from various teachers. I remember the practice of Centering Prayer in particular resonated with me, and I used to sit regularly on my prayer bench, eyes closed, deep in meditation and at peace.

Then one day, it broke. The silence stopped working for me. I suppose it wasn't quite that sudden, but as I went through a divorce and began confronting my trauma on a psychological level through therapy and journaling, I found that when I went to pray or to be quiet, I was flooded with memories and a range of emotions that simply did not allow for the quieting of the mind. Attempting to "let go gently" of intrusive thoughts became so impossible, it felt tortuous to try. Eventually, I gave up. In my contemplative group, when we practiced silence together, I allowed my mind to wander. I didn't try to be "holy" or spiritual or even inwardly still. I just thought my thoughts and felt my feelings.

Years later, I am only just beginning to renew my Centering Prayer practice, and looking back, I can see how crucial it was to my development that I gave up on it for a time. What I can see now, which wasn't clear then, is that my "meditation" practice had slowly morphed into a thinly veiled attempt to suppress my dark and heavy emotions—emotions that desperately needed to be felt and expressed if I was going to heal from my trauma. My abuser had dismissed, belittled, and ignored my feelings for years, and without recognizing it, I had become his accomplice in this self-denial. And I was using "prayer" to do it!

Fortunately, my psyche rebelled. When I tried to force my mind into silence, the psyche rang its warning bells extra loud. "Pay attention! Pay attention!" the bells said. "These feelings want to be heard." And so I relied on what I had learned from all those years wandering the wilderness—to keep going, to give thanks for any manna along the way, and to push farther into the wilderness instead of running back to Egypt.

True meditation, of course, is not intended to help us bypass feeling. But in my craving for inner peace during a difficult time, I had been trying to use meditation for my own purposes—that is, alleviation of pain—rather than allowing the practice to transport me deeper into reality, *even if* that reality was painful.

The suppression of emotion is, by nature, a patriarchal, domineering approach to the heart, and in the queendom of God, there is no place for such repressive techniques. Canadian author and dreamworker Toko-pa Turner, who is sometimes called a midwife of the psyche, writes, "We are taught to 'rise above' things like anger, anxiety, sadness—and by whatever means necessary, stay in bliss and light. This kind of bypassing is dangerous because it teaches us to not only dissociate from the multiplicity of ourselves but from the magnificent spectrum of life itself."

It is possible to misuse meditation and prayer as escape rather than entrance. Our practice becomes a way to cope with stress or help us fall asleep at night or lower our blood pressure—none of which are bad—but if that is the extent of your practice, it's like sticking your toes in the water and mistaking it for scuba diving. A rich, contemplative way of life, in my opinion, doesn't provide you relief from your problems so much as it serves as a portal to the depths of your life and then offers you the strength and stamina to endure what you discover there. This journey can be both exhilarating and terrifying, joyous and painful. In other words, if you're not experiencing the full range of human emotions, I'm not sure you're actually praying yet.

THE SUPPRESSION OF EMOTION IS, BY NATURE, A PATRIARCHAL, DOMINEERING APPROACH TO THE HEART, AND IN THE QUEENDOM OF GOD, THERE IS NO PLACE FOR SUCH REPRESSIVE TECHNIQUES.

If you are doing true inner work, you will encounter your shadow. You will become more intimate with grief. You will spend whole seasons wandering through blistering desert sands. Your soft spot for other people's pain will become softer and softer. (Or if you're an empath by nature, you might develop the skill set to remain as soft as ever but construct firmer boundaries surrounding the warm, tender center of your extraordinary sensitivity.) What I mean is, turning inward isn't always about finding peace. Sometimes it is about troubling the waters. Too often we rush to alleviate tension—in organizations, in relationships, and within ourselves. Inner work requires an ever-increasing capacity to sit with tension without resorting to quick fixes or seductive, false answers. It is called *work* for a reason.

In this chapter, I want to address inner work. Only, where does one begin? I'm not so sure there is a singular trailhead for the inner landscape. The most important thing is that you begin. Still, you will likely fare better if you can walk a trail someone has forged before you rather than having to carve one out for yourself. No one has been in your specific, individual territory before, of course, but *many* have traversed the inner world and can provide wise guidance regarding what you might encounter and how to navigate with purpose, courage, and appropriate caution. I recommend looking for some guides whose experience resonates with yours. It doesn't have to be a perfect "match" of all the same beliefs and similar stories (in fact, I'd advise against something that seems like a perfect match, as it won't much help you expand). Just look for some resonance that feels deep and true down into your bones, even if you feel a little apprehensive. Trust your gut. If someone is the wrong guide for you, you will discover it in time, or someone may be the right guide for a season, and then it will be time for you to move on. There is no shortage of guides once you are willing to see them and open yourself to them. What I am saying is, don't strike out alone. The path will feel lonely at times, but that's not the same thing as trying to Lone Ranger it. Sometimes patience is required as you wait for your next guidance; sometimes you have to step out bravely from the groupthink, not knowing if anyone will be waiting outside the circle to join you.

IF YOU'RE NOT EXPERIENCING THE FULL RANGE OF HUMAN EMOTIONS, I'M NOT SURE YOU'RE ACTUALLY PRAYING YET.

That is part of the work. But siloing yourself off from sharing the journey vulnerably with people you discern you can trust? That's the patriarchy at work in you; don't let fear keep you from connection. It is okay to ask trustworthy people for help.

Yes, yes, yes, that's all well and good about finding a guide, Kyndall, but where *do I begin?* I say, when in doubt, dive into your imagination first. So imagine now your inner landscape. Does it have rolling hills, open meadows, deep forests, lakes, rivers, streams, or oceanfront? Whatever your imagination conjures up, this is your queendom. This queendom is small in the sense that now, we are talking about just you, but this queendom is also vast because we are talking about you, and you are vast, with plenty left to be explored.

I can't see inside your queendom, but I know it is beautiful beyond reckoning and also dangerous and full of shadows. I can predict there will be many strong and steady voices who try to warn you away from exploring the far reaches of your territory. Listen to their advice to learn what their fears are, but in the end, reject the limitations of your advisors. Ultimately, barriers will not serve you.

Imagine that inside your vast queendom, there is a small village called Kingdom. It is highly controlled and relatively pleasant—at least on the surface—with manicured lawns and neat, boxy houses. Inside the village called Kingdom, it feels like the whole world. This particular set of rules, this compilation of standards, this way of being are all there is. Many people spend entire lifetimes becoming familiar with every road and alleyway of Kingdom, determined to make the best of it, to embrace and cling to it where possible, to maybe reform it where necessary. All around you, villagers seem happy with this existence. A few are dissatisfied, but all they do is complain about it, and they are not fun to be around.

Then there is you. You have this sense, almost like a knowing, that there is *more* beyond the walls of the village. Much of the time, you can ignore this knowing, but in the dark of night or in quiet moments by yourself, you feel the outer vastness calling to you. That land beyond Kingdom beckons you, but when you try to speak of it, villagers laugh or glare. "There is no such thing," some of them jeer. "It is dangerous!" others warn. The general consensus is, don't even *think* about What Lies Beyond Here.

"WAKE UP! THIS KINGDOM YOU'RE STUCK IN IS ONLY ONE TINY PORTION OF THE LAND. IT'S TIME TO START EXPLORING. YOUR QUEENDOM AWAITS."

But it keeps calling to you anyway. Here and there it tugs at you, showing up at surprising times and activating that old ache that lives in your heart and yearns from inside your soul.

This holy nudging to get moving is not inviting you to a different, grass-is-greener-on-the-other-side kingdom. It is not calling you to a new *destination*. It is inviting you to explore beyond the borders of what you've always known. It is saying, "Wake up! This kingdom you're stuck in is only one tiny portion of the land. It's time to start exploring. Your queendom awaits."

I love how Toko-pa Turner describes this moment of reckoning in her enchanting book of wisdom, *Belonging: Remembering Ourselves Home*, when she writes, "The hero or heroine in mythical tales must cross a threshold where she breaks from tradition so that she can know who she is outside the expectations of the kingdom."

Another way to think of it is like this: We are all born inside a fence. Not the same fence, but we all have our own variation of restrictions passed down to us. Some of us are given tiny little yards to explore; others are handed a large acreage. But always,

somewhere, the approved territory ends, a fence appears blocking our path, and "No Trespassing" signs are clearly and loudly
visible on the other side.

One day you will climb the fence—either because you are
inspired to do so or because you must in order to survive. Even
though it will seem that everyone has warned you that God is
not on the other side of the fence, you will go there anyway. To
your delight and surprise, you will discover God on that side of
the fence too. Eureka! What glory.

*GOD IS NOT
LIMITED TO ANY
SIDES OF ANY
FENCES. GOD IS
THE GRAVITY THAT
HOLDS YOU NO
MATTER WHERE ON
THIS ROUND GLOBE
YOU TRAVERSE.*

And so you will travel farther out
until you hit another fence. You will
likely hang out there for a long while,
thinking, "Oh! Maybe *this* is the fence.
I only thought I was crossing it before,
but now I've reached the true boundary line." You might get cold feet at
this juncture and never cross the new
fence at all. Or perhaps, once again,
you will find yourself inspired or com-
pelled to cross the boundary. To your amazement, God will be
on *that* side too.

So you will decide to go even farther out until you hit another
fence, then another, and another. If you do this enough times,
you will discover that God is not limited to any sides of any
fences. God is the gravity that holds you no matter where on
this globe you traverse.

Which is also to say, *you* are not any singular piece of your
own territory. You are the whole damn thing, so don't just hang
out in one place your whole life and expect its smallness to fulfill you.

What I am attempting to illustrate with these extended
metaphors is that the inner life is a rich landscape worthy of

exploration. I wonder: What did this imaginative experience stir up in you? What images came to mind, what feelings, what connections with your life and your unfolding story? What is your felt sense of what lies beyond the boundary line for you? Can you grant yourself the freedom to explore?

Patriarchal religion confines us to one small space within ourselves, cut off from the rest. We end up out of touch with most of humanity and out of touch with most of ourselves. Queendom: it's an inside job first. I've got to start with myself because I am my own gateway to meaningful work. No other gateway will do. I think any notion that we can change or heal the world when we've left so much of our own selves untapped is a bit ridiculous. The world needs your fullness, and so do you.

If you don't know how to get in touch with your fullness, begin with your imagination. It will take you deeper than the limitations of your analytical mind. Don't try to figure it all out or map your course in advance. Feel your way into taking another step, then another. **QUEENDOM: IT'S AN INSIDE JOB FIRST.** Release your need to control the outcome. Resist the temptation to predict what you will find or where you will go—otherwise, you will prevent yourself from seeing the paths you didn't expect.

When you do discover a path you didn't expect, take it. At the very least, walk a little ways down to see if it is a path you wish to take at this time. You can always turn around if the time isn't right. Your capacity to expand is directly related to your willingness to explore the unknown pieces of your self and, by extension, the unknown mystery of God.

I want to be clear here that traveling into the deepest realms of the self is not a self-indulgent activity but a practice that, when done well, takes you straight into the heart of the world.

I'm currently taking an antiracism course entitled "The Evil behind Your Love and Light," hosted by Dr. Frantonia Pollins. I enrolled in the course because in my line of work, I see a lot of white people meditating, deep breathing, praying, Enneagram-ing, and so forth—all with seemingly little impact on the actual structures of patriarchy and racism that damage billions of lives every day. Individuals seem to be experiencing increased health, well-being, and self-awareness, but the systems of oppression around us remain largely unchanged, which simply cannot be right. Individual wellness must be an illusion if the systems and people around me are still suffering from dis-ease. I don't mean to imply that we put our own well-being on hold when our families or our institutions refuse to catch up. What I mean is that if you are truly growing internally, it will bear external fruit, eventually. Sometimes the process itself feels mostly like chaos, and it is hard to see the good. But if you're doing your work, and your input is genuine and true, you will liberate not just yourself but others too. If the journey *only* benefits you, you're just playing on the surface of things. Your true work is still waiting to be discovered.

IF THE JOURNEY ONLY BENEFITS YOU, YOU'RE JUST PLAYING ON THE SURFACE OF THINGS. YOUR TRUE WORK IS STILL WAITING TO BE DISCOVERED.

When you fail to confront the patriarchal forces at work within you, to address white supremacy as it manifests itself in your body, to challenge your internalized homophobia—in short, to confront the demons within—you not only limit your external effectiveness; you cut off your own inner process. Dr. Pollins's course keeps reminding me that if I don't do my inner work, my external work will come out half-baked, more likely to retraumatize and damage than to heal. For example,

I might make an attempt at being "inclusive," only to find out I have been practicing tokenism instead. I might attempt to "help" those I considered vulnerable, only to realize I was operating from a white savior mindset, thereby still elevating myself over others. Or a congregation might congratulate itself for "welcoming" gay people long before its members are ready to root out their homophobia. Instead of repenting of their prejudice in a way that could truly bring healing, they pride themselves on being "loving." If we attempt outward acts of justice without doing the necessary inner work, we cause more harm than good.

This is not to say white folks or privileged folks should sit on their hands learning but never acting or speaking. But it does mean I have no business acting or speaking if I'm not also actively learning (or unlearning, as the case may be). The inner and outer worlds cannot be compartmentalized.

Any form of feminism that doesn't address the interior landscape doesn't go deep enough. That isn't to say there are not external structures to be dismantled and toppled, but if we do not also address the inner forces at work to suppress our truest selves, then external change will be temporary at best—insincere and even dangerous at worst.

ANY FORM OF FEMINISM THAT DOESN'T ADDRESS THE INTERIOR LANDSCAPE DOESN'T GO DEEP ENOUGH.

I also want to acknowledge that some external systems of oppression are so overwhelming that they *have to be* changed if the people caught inside them are to access the freedom necessary to explore the inner world. For example, if you are so strapped by poverty and trapped by the system that keeps you poor, where will you find time or resources to do deep inner healing when you are scrambling just to get food on the table? So really, it has to be both. Feminism must address the outer workings of policy, power, and privilege *and* the inner dynamics of the self and the psyche; otherwise, liberation cannot gain momentum, much less reach completion. But while it is possible to do outer work without touching the inner life, I believe it is nearly impossible to explore the inner territory in a genuine way without it impacting the outer landscape.

You will notice I am not providing you with a lot of clear-cut, concrete advice here about navigating your inner territory. For one thing, that is more than I can fit inside a single chapter of a book, and for another thing, it would be a bit fraudulent for me to pretend I *can* tell you how to do it. I can invite you to begin the journey, entice you to recommit wherever it was you left off. I can encourage you to keep going when the way is unclear, treacherous, scary, or hard and you're tempted to return to the village and the safety of fences. What I cannot do is make it happen for you. That is between you and the Spirit, and if you still feel stuck, perhaps consider the source of your resistance. Neither I nor anyone else outside of you can dive deep enough to find the genesis of your dammed-up-ness, and while guides—both human and divine—can help you, no one can do the dive or remove the blockage for you. This task is yours to do.

I AM NOT SAYING YOU HAVE TO EARN GOD'S FAVOR. I AM SAYING YOU HAVE ACCESS TO GOD'S FAVOR ALREADY—SO GO FIND OUT WHAT'S BEEN BLOCKING YOUR ACCESS ALL THIS TIME.

There is this mistaken notion in Christianity that as recipients of grace, we are passive, which can lead either to apathy or to entitlement. On the contrary, receptivity requires an active presence that passiveness does not entertain. I am not saying you have to earn God's favor. I am saying you have access to God's favor already—so go find out what's been blocking your access all this time. Chances are, the thing in your way is you. It may be that the barricade was first erected by some external, abusive force outside yourself and beyond your control, but how have you *internalized* that blockade so that it has become a living element of your own psyche? Don't blame yourself for the obstruction, but don't abdicate yourself of all responsibility for removing it either.

While I cannot prescribe exactly the steps you will need to take, I can describe certain elements of the journey. I'd start by attempting to name the More-ness that exists beyond your village boundaries, but already I would probably be overreaching. Let me start instead by naming my own More-ness and the More-ness I have witnessed others uncover, all while recognizing that names, while incredibly useful, also have a tendency to fall short. If these names don't work for you, ask yourself why. Is it because the name itself is threatening to your limited Kingdom? If so, it may be just the name you've needed. Is it because another, different name feels more authentic, more true, to your genuine experience of the unknown? Then may you feel all the permission you need to write your own names.

One name I would give to my own experience of More-ness is Divine Feminine. We live in a world that is hostile to the feminine, has often forced her into hiding (think witch hunts, think male-only clergy, think the exaltation of logic over intuition, think the ravaging of Mother Earth, think violence against women's bodies, think colonialism, think exclusively masculine pronouns for God, think force and dominion over collaborative creativity). We have divorced the feminine from its sacred origins and its rightful identification with divinity. This greatly harms both women and men—not to mention how it erases and denigrates the existence of anyone who doesn't identify solidly with the gender binary to begin with.

For me, once I left the strict boundaries of village, of Kingdom, I found Her, and it was life altering. Whether the name *Divine Feminine* (or Great Mother or Goddess or Wise Woman or Sophia, etc.) resonates immediately with you or not, I want to be clear that this is by no means a name worth reclaiming for female-identifying persons only. In fact, it is crucial for men to reacquaint themselves with the feminine. Patriarchy has tried to stamp it out of all of us, but for men especially, the erasure can be severe and challenging to reverse. To use Jungian language, to become an integrated individual, a man *must* get in touch with his anima. I would go so far as to say that this integration is non-negotiable for the healing of both the soul and the world.

ONCE I LEFT THE STRICT BOUNDARIES OF VILLAGE, OF KINGDOM, I FOUND HER, AND IT WAS LIFE ALTERING.

In a somewhat similar way, you could say that women need to get reacquainted with their animus energy, or the sacred masculine within, so that we can all retrieve a balance between these two energies; *however*, it is usually critical for a woman to encounter the divine feminine *first* because before she can uncover and restore balance to her sacred masculine, she must—with the help of the feminine divine—slay the patriarchal, domineering god that has been masquerading in her life as "Father God" all this time. Only when he is gone or at least quieted can the divine feminine and sacred masculine meet together as their real selves and join in union as equal partners.

I want to acknowledge here that the language I am using is overtly binary and therefore may be too constricting to be useful for some of you, and that's okay. You don't have to use my words to name your More-ness. I do believe that as long as we live in an environment that is so largely shaped by a binary understanding of gender, with a distorted emphasis placed on the masculine, talking about recovering and restoring the feminine will continue to be essential to the conversation. Perhaps the day will come when such categories no longer serve us because we will have evolved beyond our need for them, in which case, I am confident the More-ness will never cease to run out of names. For now, names like *Divine Feminine* and *Queendom* say a lot that is worth saying.

There are other names I find helpful too—names like Mystery, Becoming, the Unknown, the Unconscious, the Dance, the Spirit, the Deep, the Holy. Sometimes simply the Universe. It is impossible to find a name that captures all of it, and yet names provide us some handles to hold, a language for speaking about the ineffable, and a vehicle of communication between souls. Whatever name you may use, I pray that you travel beyond the boundaries long enough to find Her.

AS LONG AS WE LIVE IN AN ENVIRONMENT THAT IS SO LARGELY SHAPED BY A BINARY UNDERSTANDING OF GENDER, WITH A DISTORTED EMPHASIS PLACED ON THE MASCULINE, TALKING ABOUT RECOVERING AND RESTORING THE FEMININE WILL CONTINUE TO BE ESSENTIAL TO THE CONVERSATION.

I think about when naming is used as a sort of ownership, like giving indigenous people "Christian" names as a way to claim them. This is decidedly *not* a kind of naming the queendom inside you will tolerate. She *allows* herself to be named by you because She wants to relate to you. If you try to use one of

Her many names to control Her or box Her in, you can be certain She will stop showing up. She is not yours to manage. She is Her own wild, untamable mystery, gracious enough to allow your exploration—*if* you maintain your reverence.

How's that for a map? I think it is the most I can give you, the truest I can give you. May you journey deeper and deeper into the mystery of your wilderness. Traveling mercies, beloved. I am cheering you on.

CHAPTER 4

Pull Up a Chair

Now seems about the right time to talk about Micah and his mother from Judges 17, don't you think? In case you didn't learn this story in Sunday school, let me do a quick recap: A woman's silver is stolen. She utters a curse aloud, perhaps not knowing the thief is standing within earshot. It must have been some hell of a curse because the thief is sufficiently scared into returning the silver.

When the thief—that is, *her son*—returns the money, she responds with blessings. She does not hold her son accountable for his actions. She cries out, "The Lord bless you, my son!" and then she takes two hundred of the eleven hundred pieces of silver and turns them into an idol because, well, who knows why, but that is what she does. Her son, Micah, is enthusiastic about this. He makes an ephod and some household gods. He needs a priest, so naturally, he installs one of his own sons (I assume because it was convenient). The narrator reports—and this is important—"In those days there was no king in Israel; all the people did what was right in their own eyes."

The story continues. A wandering Levite shows up at Micah's doorstep looking for a place to stay. Micah offers, "Stay with me, and be to me a father and a priest, and I will give you ten pieces of silver a year, a set of clothes, and your living." Ten pieces of silver per year puts into perspective just how much Micah stole from his mother when he took *eleven hundred* pieces. The Levite agrees to stay, and Micah assumes, "Now I know that the Lord will prosper me, because the Levite has become my priest."

And thus concludes chapter 17. Weird story, right? While you might not have heard much about this story before, it represents a significant turning point in Judges. Throughout the book, we find this repeated refrain: "The Israelites again did what was evil *in the sight of the Lord.*" But in chapter 17, the description changes: "All the people did what was right *in their own eyes.*" God is no longer a part of it, as if God isn't even watching. Or perhaps the people have simply forgotten that God is watching.

The story of Micah, his mother, and the Levite, though strange, serves as an illustration of the point: "All the people did what was right in their own eyes." Micah, motivated by greed, steals from his own mother. When he hears her curse, he returns the money. This time, I assume, he is motivated by fear of the curse. In other words, Micah looks out for Micah. Then he and his mother begin a practice of worship—only none of it makes any sense. They make an idol, and Micah appoints his own son as a priest but then hires a Levite to do the job when he happens to wander by. The whole thing feels willy-nilly, unplanned, and unexamined. They just did what was right in their own eyes, you might say.

Micah, though, believes God will prosper him for all of this. However, things do not unfold quite the way Micah expects. If you keep reading into chapter 18, the tribe of Dan is on the look-out for some good land. They send spies to explore the land, and while they are traveling, they stay with Micah. They ask the Levite what he is doing and who brought him there. Usually we think of priests as called by God, but this priest appears as willy-nilly about things as Micah. He answers their questions—I imagine with a shrug—saying, "Micah did such and such for me, and hired me, and I have become his priest." The Danite spies then want the Levite to inquire of God whether their mission will succeed. Without actually asking God or even pausing to think about it, the Levite replies, "Go in peace. The mission you are on is *under the eye of the Lord*." Interesting choice of words—"eye of the Lord"—isn't it, since everyone is doing what is right in their own eyes?

The spies of the Danite clan then discover the city of Laish, where, the text says, "they observed the people who were there living securely . . . quiet and unsuspecting, lacking nothing on earth, and possessing wealth." And so eventually, six hundred armed men from the Danite tribe march to Laish.

On their way to overtake Laish, the Danites again stop at Micah's house, but this time, they aim to take his idol. The Levite priest asks them what they are doing, but they reason with him, "Is it better for you to be priest to the house of one person, or to be priest to a tribe and clan in Israel?" The Levite seems to think they make a good point, so he steals the idol and ephod himself and goes with the Danites. Micah attempts to chase after them, but when Micah sees that they are too strong and he cannot win, he turns back. Ironically, the thief returns home a victim of theft.

Meanwhile, the text reports, the Danites, "having taken what Micah had made, and the priest who belonged to him, came to Laish, to a people quiet and unsuspecting, put them to the sword, and burned down the city."

Um, what? Why is this story included in the Bible? Placed near the end of Judges, it is a picture of how haphazard and unfocused the people have become. The escapades with the silver idol may sound silly, but are they really so different from our own world? Wealth drives Micah, drives his mother, drives the

Levite, drives the Danites to attack Laish. In the story, religion appears to be made up on a whim, and even the priest has no moral center, no grounding. God's name is used to sanction the robbery of an entire city, but God makes no real appearance in the story except on the lips of men attempting to justify violence. Does this sound far-fetched to you or eerily familiar? God's name being used in vain to sanctify acts of terror and greed sounds like something pulled right from the modern playbook.

The line that appears in verse 6 of this story, "In those days there was no king in Israel; all the people did what was right in their own eyes," is the same exact line with which the book ends: "In those days there was no king in Israel; all the people did what was right in their own eyes." You may remember the account of the concubine whose body was chopped into pieces at the end of Judges. Micah's story is the precursor to true horror. He is like the warning light no one heeds. There is danger ahead, but there is no relationship with God to slow the tide. There is only this relationship to a false god and the worship of wealth. Every facet of the narrative centers on what someone can get for themselves. Everyone did as they saw fit . . . there was no higher power, no point of focus, no gravity, no center. From beginning to end, decisions are rash, random, and self-absorbed.

GOD'S NAME BEING USED IN VAIN TO SANCTIFY ACTS OF TERROR AND GREED SOUNDS LIKE SOMETHING PULLED RIGHT FROM THE MODERN PLAYBOOK.

I bring this story up in part because it is not uncommon for those of us who are exploring the great mystery rather than staying put in the kingdom to be accused of merely "doing what is right in our own eyes," of making up spirituality, of following the whims of society, or of creating God in our image. If you remove the boundaries, how do you prevent yourself from wandering into evil? How do you know your "experiences" of the divine aren't just a figment of your imagination or a product of culture or, even worse, something planted there by the devil? What if we aren't any better than Micah, his so-called priest, or the Danites who slaughter the people of Laish?

Again and again, the patriarchy will use stories like this one to warn you: "Do not trust yourself! Your self is dangerous and deceitful, and if you listen to your own inner wisdom, you will be led astray. This is why you must look to external authority, like the Bible or religious leaders or doctrine to guide you. What if your inner desire is to *murder* someone?" And they might say this to dissuade you from following your own wisdom: "You cannot just follow your own inclinations, see? You will get yourself into trouble."

Here is why the patriarchy's argument is no good: Which do you think is more dangerous? An inner desire is to kill someone (which hopefully you will be too sensible to act on) or a command from God to kill via the authority of the men who represent him? If *the religious authorities* demand violence, such as during the Crusades, the Inquisition, or other wars and genocides throughout human history, there is a very real and serious danger that other people will be persuaded to enact violence. They might not even feel compelled personally, but they have been conditioned to believe the wisdom of the external authorities, even when it goes against their very nature. Note that the Danites *did* consult a religious authority—that is, the Levite—and he gave them his blessing (offered in God's name) to massacre a town. The problem isn't that internal authority is inherently

AGAIN AND AGAIN, THE PATRIARCHY WILL USE STORIES LIKE THIS ONE TO WARN YOU.

more dangerous than external authority; the problem is that life can be dangerous, and discernment is *always* required. But sometimes we farm that discernment work out to somebody else who claims to be an expert. Or we make choices based not on the true selves we have uncovered by doing deep work but on the demands of the repressed shadow we have failed to examine by daylight.

The trouble isn't internal authority versus external authority; it is a lack of discernment. When Judges 17 claims that "all the people did what was right in their own

THERE IS NO "HEAD OF THE TABLE" IN THE QUEENDOM; THE TABLE IS ROUND.

eyes," the predicament wasn't that they dared to go against the authority of leaders. The problem was that they weren't seeing clearly—not because "common" eyes are inherently worse than "authority" eyes but because they weren't interested in honing their vision. It's like driving a car while wearing the wrong pair of prescription glasses and choosing not to care about who you might endanger.

What has happened for so many of us who grew up in religious systems, particularly patriarchal ones, is that we were taught to listen to external authority *to the exclusion of* internal knowing. We were taught that the "heart is deceitful above all things, and desperately wicked." We were taught not to indulge our doubts or questions, not to feel our feelings, and not to listen to intuition or our truest selves, especially when they ran counter to the status quo.

I think it is time to say "no more" to that nonsense. Our inner knowing is vital, wise, necessary. The way I see it, there is no "head of the table" in the queendom; the table is round. That means the marginalized have just as much of a voice as the powerful. (What if, for example, the Danites had consulted the children of Laish before they went to war?) It also means *you* have just as much of a voice as any voice of external authority.

Is it a good idea to listen deeply to the wisdom of others, to include and invite their perspectives, to seek out expertise, and to take alternative viewpoints seriously? Yes. Absolutely. But if you marginalize your own voice in the process, you are no better than a tyrant yourself. Everyone deserves a seat at the table, including you.

Of course, there is a stark difference between the empowered belief that your voice does, in fact, belong and the privileged perspective that you are entitled to have a say all the time, in every context, and before you've done your homework. One attitude speaks from a place of authentic inner authority. It is the kind of *author*-ity that recognizes your right to author your own story, free from coercion. The other kind of attitude speaks from the arrogant prerogative to coerce others as afforded you by your status, color, gender, able-bodiedness, and so on. If you are speaking in a way that defends your own privilege, I would suggest that you are not only perpetuating harm toward

BUT IF YOU MARGINALIZE YOUR OWN VOICE IN THE PROCESS, YOU ARE NO BETTER THAN A TYRANT YOURSELF. EVERYONE DESERVES A SEAT AT THE TABLE, INCLUDING YOU.

the marginalized people around you; you are also perpetuating harm toward the marginalized parts of yourself. Any exclusive behavior on the outside reflects an inner fissure that dominates and subjugates not only other people but also the best and truest parts of yourself.

How do you know whether you are speaking out of your privilege or out of your authenticity? I would suggest you go within and imagine your inner round table. Who is present?

Who has been silenced? Who has been kept from the table altogether? Does your grief have a voice? Does your fear get to speak alongside your confidence? Does your joy have any say? What about your desire and longing? Your apprehension, your enthusiasm, your passion, your hesitation? Your guilt as well as your sense of being beloved by God? Your shadow and your light? Have you boiled a pot of tea for your anger, brought out the coffee and sugar for your hurt feelings, extended hospitality to that part of yourself you don't really like? The more inner colleagues you bring to the table and allow to speak, the more authentic and genuine your outer speech will become. Your various inner voices can temper and balance one another rather than boxing each other out. You will be able to hear the full choir of your wisdom.

SITTING AT THE "HEAD" OF THE TABLE IN THE BOARDROOM WILL DISQUIET YOU RATHER THAN EXCITE YOU. YOU WILL WISH FOR ROUND TABLES.

If you do this on the inside, it will become more natural on the outside. You will be quicker to ask, "Wait, who is missing from this conversation?" You will notice when leadership is homogenous, and the homogeny will feel alarming. Your body will begin to reject the demands of conformity. Your capacity to be challenged by those with less institutional power than you will increase. Sitting at the "head" of the table in the boardroom will disquiet you rather than excite you. You will wish for round tables. If it is within your power to do so, you will request and demand rounder tables. When someone without status has something to say, your inclination will be to stop and listen, and listen closely. When someone new shows up, you will pull up a chair.

Let's consider again Micah, his stolen idol, and the Danite conquest. The book of Judges is intended to set us up for the introduction of the Israelite monarchy. It's not just that "all the people did what was right in their own eyes." The narrator says quite often, "There was no king in Israel." By the end of the book, the author of Judges wants you as a reader to feel desperate for somebody to bring order to the chaos, hope to the despair, humanity to the inhumane, and leadership to the anarchy. The end of Judges is the perfect literary segue into the book of 1 Samuel and the eventual kingship of David.

Of course, if we zoom out even further, in the wider context of the whole Bible, kingship creates more problems than it solves. Some kings are good(ish), but some are bad, and some are *really* bad. People thought kings would be an upgrade from the judges. I mean, if your bar is Samson, yeah, okay, but that's a pretty low bar. Kings, it turns out, are not the solution.

It is worth noting that in the book of Samuel, a king is not God's idea; it is the people who demand a king. God tries to warn them through the prophet Samuel that kings will be greedy and will take, take, take, but the people do not listen. When times are chaotic and painful, we crave order, crave authority, crave simplicity. Fear told the people they needed a savior in the form of a warrior, a king, a fighter.

We see these fears at work in our culture today. Sometimes people look to a particular personality to lead them; others look to an airtight philosophy of some kind. One popular choice today is the king called Fundamentalism; we could name several others. People look to kings to rule over them and make all things right, simple, black and white. Understandably, they are afraid of what happens when everyone does what is "right in their own eyes," and so they gravitate toward what feels secure.

That is, they farm out their own responsibility for discernment because they are scared.

Queendom people seek to shed ourselves of toxic authoritarianism. But where does that leave us? With the same willy-nilly, freelance religion of Micah and his mother, the Levite and the Danites? Do we all just do what is right in our own eyes? Are our critics right about us? We just drift along with the changing seasons of the culture?

THE QUEENDOM IS NOT MOTIVATED BY GREED, BY WEALTH, OR BY SECURITY. IT IS MOTIVATED BY LOVE.

I would suggest no, queendom faith is deeper and truer and purer than that. It can be challenging to hold on to faith when you are someone who is open to questions, open to doubt and uncertainty, open to criticisms about how religion has done real damage to people. If you stay open, the kingdom will insist you are doing it wrong. They might tell you you're going to hell. Or you need to repent. Your rejection of certainty is a rejection of the faith. You just do whatever you want, whatever you think is right, and call it a faith.

But this is not true. The queendom is not motivated by greed, by wealth, or by security. It is motivated by love, and love is a very different driving force than what drove Micah or the Danites. You have rejected the king of external authority not so you can be king but because the mystery of the queendom defies kingship, and your soul requires reverence for the mystery. You refuse to call your own limited perspective the "eyes of God," and at the same time, you take what your own eyes see seriously because it is God who gave you eyes. You allow what you see into your heart.

Micah had no center. The priest in the story had no center. The Danites had no center. They couldn't properly see because their eyeballs had no connection to their hearts. They saw silver, gold, wealth; they *couldn't* see the humanity of the people they ran over to acquire and accumulate. None of them had done their inner work.

Have you ever been to the eye doctor, peering into the machine while she flips the lenses and asks you over and over which is better, one or two? Two or one? I find this maddening because I'm always second-guessing myself. *I think one was better. No wait, maybe it was two. Fuck. What if I get this wrong, and why am I sweating?*

In the end, I have to trust the process. That by answering as honestly as I can, even when I'm not sure, eventually I will arrive at the right—or nearly right—prescription. I think maybe discernment is a little bit like this. It's not that we get to have clarity all the time. We do the best we can, and we stay in the chair, even if we're sweating and want to leave. We keep peering, we keep asking ourselves, "Which one?" We don't just pick up a random pair of glasses as if any old prescription will do. We don't borrow the glasses of our mentor or our pastor or our guru or our parents and assume those will be just fine for us without any adjustments. We look deep within and find our center. And ever so softly the center whispers, "One. Now two. This time it's one again."

It's never quick. It's never without some self-questioning. It usually endures some outside interference. But when we listen from our center, every voice at the table is equidistant and able to be heard, and that means we are guided well and holistically.

This poem by Rumi has saved my life more than once:

This being human is a guest house.
Every morning a new arrival.
A joy, a depression, a meanness,

some momentary awareness comes
as an unexpected visitor.
Welcome and entertain them all!
Even if they are a crowd of sorrows,
who violently sweep your house
empty of its furniture,
still, treat each guest honorably.
He may be clearing you out
for some new delight.
The dark thought, the shame, the malice.
meet them at the door laughing and invite them in.
Be grateful for whatever comes.
because each has been sent
as a guide from beyond.

When you are confused about what to do or which way to go, pull up another chair. Listen to whoever shows up. Ground yourself in love. Keep widening the table. Start with the table inside you.

CHAPTER 5

Honestly

If it had been up to Jesus's disciples, Mary Magdalene would not have had a seat at the table. In fact, they quite literally overlook her in Acts 1, when they gather together to choose a replacement for Judas. She is presumably in the room when the successor is chosen, but the eleven nominate two men we readers have never heard of before.

By the time the disciples pass her over as the qualified replacement for Judas, Mary Magdalene is a veteran at having her voice dismissed but using it anyway. After all, she is one of the first to witness Jesus's resurrection, but listen to how she is treated by the men: "It was Mary Magdalene, Joanna, Mary the mother of James, and the other women with them who told this to the apostles. But these words seemed to them an idle tale, and they did not believe them."

Mary Magdalene, Joanna, and the other women have just witnessed *the biggest event* in Christianity, but when they attempt to tell the male disciples the Huge Important News, the men mansplain their story away. "It is just an idle tale," they say, or, depending on your translation, it seemed to them like folly, like pure nonsense, like insanity, like BS.

Fortunately, Peter decides to check things out for himself. Thank goodness for him, right? The only man curious enough about what the women were saying to go take a look. But even after Peter sees the empty tomb, the text says he went away, wondering to himself what had happened. He still didn't believe the women's explanation of the empty tomb. In Luke's account, it isn't until Jesus appears to the two travelers on the road to Emmaus—at least one of whom was a man—that the story starts to gain credibility.

AND THE REFUSAL TO BELIEVE WOMEN EXTENDS BEYOND THE CHURCH. IT EXISTS IN OUR WORKPLACES, IN OUR HOMES, ON OUR CAMPUSES, AND IN OUR ORGANIZATIONS.

We still have churches and denominations that insist women cannot preach, even though in the gospels, women were the first to preach the resurrection. We still have religious leaders today who claim that men have special access to God, even though in all four Gospels, it is women to whom the angels appear and proclaim Christ has risen. And the refusal to believe women extends beyond the church. It exists in our workplaces, in our homes, on our campuses, and in our organizations—when a woman claims she has expertise, when a woman has an idea at the board meeting, when a woman says she is being harassed or that she feels unsafe or that she deserves a raise. This is why you might read about the disciples dismissing the women's story and not even bat an eye. This refusal to believe them is normal, everyday gender dynamics. Nothing surprising. It's not just that the resurrection is unbelievable. After all, Jesus did loads of unbelievable stuff, including raising people from the dead. The problem with their story about Jesus's resurrection is that there are no male eyewitnesses, and thus the story cannot be trusted.

In fact, we are so averse to believing women that we fabricate additions to their stories in order to cast further doubt on their credibility. For example, you may have grown up hearing and believing that Mary Magdalene was a prostitute even though the Bible *never says* she was a prostitute. All we know about her past from the Bible is that Jesus once cast seven demons out of her, and it doesn't say it was a demon of prostitution.

But throughout the centuries, the rumors about Mary Magdalene's sordid past solidified into something we accept as true so that when the male disciples do not believe her testimony about Christ, we might be inclined to think, "Well, why should they? Look at who she'd been." But I would like to suggest that if they were going to believe anyone at all, Mary Magdalene should have been their top pick. If we reclaim her from the stuff the church has made up about her and return to the biblical text, who is she really? Along with Joseph of Arimathea and Nicodemus, she accompanies Jesus's body to the grave long after the prominent disciples have fled the scene. Along with the other women, she is the first to visit the tomb, and in John's Gospel, she is the only one to stay at the tomb and encounter the risen Christ herself.

Unlike Peter, who denies Jesus; unlike Judas, who betrays him; unlike the disciples who fall asleep in the garden and the disciples who flee the scene at Jesus's arrest; and unlike the disciples who lock themselves in an upper room for fear of the authorities, Mary Magdalene stays, she persists. By all accounts, she remains the most faithful of all the disciples. She continues to follow Jesus, even when he is dead. If anyone should be trusted in this particular story, it is Mary Magdalene—faithful disciple, loyal friend, feminine witness.

In many of the Eastern Orthodox icons depicting Mary Magdalene, you'll often find her holding a red egg in her hand. That is because legend has it that after the ascension of Christ, Mary Magdalene gained an audience with the emperor in Rome. She used an egg from the dinner table to illustrate the resurrection, saying that Christ rose from the grave like a chick bursting from an egg. Tiberius Caesar scoffed at her (sound familiar?) and said that there was as much chance of a human returning from the dead as there was for an egg to turn red. And what do you know? Immediately, the egg turned red. Once again the men in power didn't believe her. Once again she proved them wrong. In Luke's Gospel, of course, it is not just Mary Magdalene alone but a whole chorus of women proclaiming the good news, but still, the other disciples do not believe them. Even so, it doesn't stop the women from proclamation.

One of my favorite parts of the Mary Magdalene story happens in the Gospel of John when she encounters the risen Christ alone in the garden. Some translations have Jesus saying to her "Don't touch me," but really, what he says is "Don't cling to me" or "Don't hold to me." In other words, "You cannot just stay here with me, Mary. You *must* go out and tell the people what has happened."

I came out of a Southern Baptist tradition in which women were not allowed to preach or pastor or lead. So when I arrived at seminary and could say out loud "I am called to be a pastor" and no one cringed or recoiled or argued, I thought it was pretty amazing. I could share my sense of being called, and people believed me. It was like a balm for my soul after experiencing repeated disbelief and rejection.

But a few years in, after I had healed a bit from the decades of a church that said God made women less-than on purpose, I started noticing some things about my new supportive environment. There was only one woman on faculty at the seminary, for example. She was also, at the time I began my education, the only person of color on the faculty. So if you didn't take her class—and many people didn't because she had a reputation for being tough—then you could complete your entire theological education and never hear a female scholar's perspective or a person of color's perspective. All our textbooks were written by men. There was a single day in a church history course where we learned about Christian feminism—a couple pages in a textbook written by a man, explaining feminist theology as if the movement could be captured in a few short paragraphs. These paragraphs left the impression that feminism was some fringe theological view that could scarcely be called Christian and not—as I came to discover later, on my own—this dynamic, universal, vibrant, Pentecost-type movement of the Spirit with the power to dismantle systemic evils and awaken new life in battered souls.

After graduating seminary, I reflected on the fact that we had chapel every week, but on average, I saw about one woman in the chapel pulpit per semester. At first, I was so thrilled to see a woman preaching at all that this seemed incredible. But in retrospect, it struck me as very sad that an institution claiming to support women in leadership was only willing to share the power of the pulpit with a woman once a semester. Students don't even go to every chapel service, so in theory, you could graduate seminary and still have never heard a woman preach. You could attend a school that affirmed women and leave that place entirely unexposed to the influence of a woman's voice and perspective.

Like, what if we women witnessed a resurrection? We don't even have a platform to tell you, and if we do get a platform, it is so freaking rare, you are preconditioned to see us as outside the norm. And if we start talking about what we have seen and what we have heard and what it is really like walking in our shoes, you're predisposed to think we might be nuts—that it's nonsense, an idle tale, an overreaction; or that we're rude; or that we're just making stuff up because we're so emotional, we can't think straight.

I decided to write a letter to my seminary. I recruited several other alumnae to write it with me, and we kindly and politely asked that the seminary consider our request for equal representation of women and men in chapel. We didn't touch on the almost exclusively male textbooks or male faculty. We kept it simple—an easily attainable goal. We made it so easy that we even compiled a list of twenty-two women they might consider. For each and every potential preacher, we provided her contact information so it would be as effortless as possible to reach out to her.

Before too long, we received a response from the dean. He thanked us for our letter and said we were right, that they would work on this. *Wow, what a difference it can make*, I thought, *when women overcome their fears and hesitations and advocate for themselves.*

The following semester, I eagerly went online to check the chapel schedule. I scrolled through the names of the preachers in the lineup—male, male, male, male. There were two women total on the list that semester. I suppose if you are a glass-half-full type, you would say they doubled their female representation in chapel. But I was no longer a glass-half-full kind of gal. I was waking up to the fact that I had merely moved from the hostile patriarchy of Southern Baptist land to the benevolent patriarchy of my new territory. It was the kind of patriarchy that allows you in the room but doesn't listen to what you are saying. The kind of patriarchy that hands you a glass of water as if it were a great act of generosity to share their water with you. When you go to drink it, it's not half full at all. There are a few drops in the bottom of the glass, drops contaminated by the residue of sexism, and for this you are expected to be grateful—because at least they weren't shunning you completely.

The turning point for me personally came a few years after we had sent the letter to the dean and no one on our list was ever invited to preach. A current seminary student who led the school's women in ministry group came to one of my female colleagues, and she was *so* excited because she had talked to the dean about having better representation of women in chapel, and he said that was a great idea. *He just wanted her to get him a list of names.*

I WAS WAKING UP TO THE FACT THAT I HAD MERELY MOVED FROM THE HOSTILE PATRIARCHY OF SOUTHERN BAPTIST LAND TO THE BENEVOLENT PATRIARCHY OF MY NEW TERRITORY.

Suddenly it dawned on me that *my* letter to the seminary wasn't the first one. I was part of a chorus of women who had been saying for years that we—men and women—we need more women's voices, and they hadn't listened to any of us. They might have *said* they believed us, but their actions spoke louder than their words.

Soon after, the seminary hosted a preaching conference, and out of seventeen speakers, *two* of them were women. When we inquired about the lineup, we were told there just weren't enough women in the field to ask. As events like these continued to transpire with regularity, no matter how politely we advocated for change, my friend Rev. Natalie Webb and I realized that we could no longer wait on the institution to invite more women. We were just going to have to invite them ourselves.

And so we cofounded Nevertheless She Preached, a preaching event designed to elevate and center the voices of women on the margins. We didn't know if we could actually pull it off. We wanted to organize a major preaching conference, but we had only five weeks to make it happen—not to mention no money or venue—*and* we had been told countless times that there just weren't enough women in our field to invite as speakers. But we were determined to try. Our measuring stick was this: if we could secure two dynamic preachers to come speak, we would proceed with planning our event. We extended invitations to various women speakers, explaining what we were doing and assuring them that we *hoped* to be able to pay them, but to begin with, we didn't actually have a budget.

Women said yes, over and over. We had to keep expanding our schedule to accommodate nine keynote speakers from across denominations and across the country. This was around the time that the phrase "Nevertheless, she persisted" became popular after Senator Mitch McConnell used it in reference to Senator Elizabeth Warren, and so we decided to call our event Nevertheless She Preached. We sold T-shirts as a fundraiser, and within five weeks, we had raised twenty thousand dollars. My friend Rev. Heather Mooney designed our logo, and the letters of *she* in Nevertheless She Preached were formed using the names of women who had preached throughout Christian history. We weren't just connecting ourselves to one another; we were connecting back to the long tradition of our bold and eloquent female ancestors.

The conference was a huge success, and I was utterly blown away by what felt like a real-life miracle—all these powerful women sharing space and a platform together. Surrounded by women at the conference, I realized that the patriarchy had been keeping us from one another in all kinds of ways and with all kinds of lies and with all sorts of competitiveness, as if we had to beat one another out for the limited number of spaces available to us. But when we created our own space, there was room for everybody, and everybody had a voice, and as a result, the Holy Spirit was set loose.

It turned out we weren't the only women who felt alone and dismissed. It was a universal, ecumenical experience of women everywhere. We had struck a chord, and people responded. On the last day of that first conference, overflowing with my new sense of shared sisterhood, I said, "The myth of our isolation has been forever shattered for me."

Isolation is an effective tactic of the patriarchy. I am reminded of a friend I know whose preaching professor told her it was best not to get too close with one of the country's well-known female preachers, even though they had a personal connection, because, he said, she was a little too radical, and it could ruin my friend's career to be associated with *her*. Another colleague of mine was "warned" multiple times by male leaders that she wouldn't get along with other female clergy. Countless clergywomen I know have been sent by their denominations to rural, isolated areas to serve dying churches without support or resources.

In order for the queendom to thrive, we not only have to tell the truth and tell it often; we have to band together with those who will tell the truth with us and beside us, those who have told the truth long before us, and those who will continue to tell it after us.

In 1896, a German collector discovered in an antiquities market in Cairo the ancient replica of an even older document now known to the modern world as the Gospel of Mary Magdalene. It was originally written around the same time as the Gospel of John, but it was lost to humanity for over a thousand years. In it, Mary Magdalene has clear prominence among the disciples, which matches the biblical tradition about her if we read the Bible honestly.

There is this moment in her gospel when Peter says to Mary Magdalene, "Sister, we know that the Savior greatly loved you above all other women, so tell us what you remember of his words that we ourselves do not know or perhaps have never heard." Peter recognizes her as someone with special knowledge that he himself does not possess and must learn by listening to her.

A PROPHET MAY NOT BE ACCEPTED IN HIS HOMETOWN, BUT A PROPHETESS IS WELCOME, WELL, ALMOST NOWHERE.

Of course, after she obliges Peter and teaches the disciples what she knows, Andrew replies like this: "Say what you will about all that she has said to us, *I* for one do not believe that the Savior said such things to her, for they are strange and appear to differ from the rest of his teachings." Sound familiar? And then Peter, who originally asked Mary Magdalene to speak, decides to go with his brother Andrew on this one, asking, "Would the Savior speak these things to a woman in private without sharing them so that we too might hear? Should we listen to her at all, and did he choose her over us because she is more worthy than we are?"

It is Levi who comes to her defense, saying, "You have always been quick to anger, Peter, and now you are questioning her in exactly the same manner, treating this woman as if she were an enemy. If the Savior considered her worthy, who are you to reject her? He knew her completely and loved her faithfully. We should be ashamed of ourselves. We should be clothed with the cloak of true humility and following his command announce the good news without burdening it further with rules or laws he himself did not give us."

And the gospel ends this way: "After Levi had said this, they departed and began to teach, proclaiming the Good News." And I presume when it says they began to teach and preach, that meant all of them, including Mary Magdalene, who despite being questioned and disbelieved over and over again, kept preaching nevertheless.

In my experience, many men in leadership positions are too uncomfortable to name the patriarchy that still finds fertile breeding ground in their organizations and seminaries and churches. Good intentioned though they may be, their silence (and their silencing) props up the systemic sexism that limits the amplification of women's voices. That is why, in the queendom, we build large platforms, pass out megaphones, shine spotlights, join choirs and protests and chants, perform street poetry, create art, and communicate by any means necessary in order to say the true things that will make people uncomfortable. Because the status quo never went down in comfort, and nothing wounded ever gets healed by keeping it hidden. A prophet may not be accepted in his hometown, but a prophetess is welcome, well, almost nowhere. She is the truth in woman's flesh, and that is just too much word inside too much flesh. When given the chance, the world will crucify her.

I want to return here to the story of the murdered concubine I mentioned in chapter 2, because if we are going to be truthtellers, we have to tell stories like hers. She wasn't able to tell her own story, but someone had the guts, horrible as the story was, to write it down so it wouldn't be forgotten. Yet over and over through the years, churches and Christians and pastors forget to retell it, but I have committed myself to her, to telling the truth about her, to offering her my sisterhood, posthumously. Consider her with me. Consider her truth. Consider her flesh.

Her name is not known to us. This woman whose body was handled by every tribe of Israel somehow remains nameless, though she must have been the most talked-about woman in the nation. Before the days of the printing press, he used her flesh and bone and made a tabloid out of her. Can you imagine anybody who *wasn't* talking about her? "I heard the tribe of Gad got her feet and ankles. The tribe of Reuben received her left arm. Judah got the head."

It sounds utterly disgusting and totally inappropriate for dinner table talk, but you know as well as I that people are drawn to scandal like flies to a picnic. Everyone was talking about her, even if they didn't know her name. It's hard to ignore the bloody stump of a leg that shows up on the village doorstep after all. She was known and examined and discussed by all—yet not really known at all.

The beginning of her story is really quite remarkable because *she leaves him.* If you think divorce is hard now, try being a woman in ancient Israel. Leaving was not an option for women in those days, but somehow—we don't know how—she *makes* it an option for herself. When the story begins, she is a very independent woman. Why she left depends on which ancient manuscript you read. The Hebrew and Syriac claim she played the harlot, while the Greek and Old Latin say she became angry and left. Whatever the reason, she has to travel a great distance (alone perhaps) to return to the one place she might be safe after leaving her husband—her father's house. We don't know her exact reasons for leaving—undoubtedly, they were good ones for her to take such a huge risk—but whatever her motive, she is a woman who spoke her truth. We don't know if she said the words out loud to him, "I'm leaving," or if she took off without warning because a silent departure was the only way a woman could escape. Either way, her actions spoke volumes.

She stays with her father for four full months, but after all that time has passed, her husband decides he wants her back. We have been conditioned by Hollywood to think that when a man chases after a woman who leaves him, it is romantic. In reality, it is a violation of her truth. She said she didn't want to be with him anymore, and he ignored it. Another name for this is stalking.

Some translations say he "set out after her to convince her to come back," but a better translation of the Hebrew would be to say he set out to "speak to her heart." Biblical scholar Phyllis Trible notes, "The words 'speak to her heart' connote reassurance, comfort, loyalty, and love." There is at least a hint of romantic intention at the story's start. However, once he arrives at her father's house, the only conversation that occurs is between the two men as they eat and visit with each other for five days, after which the Levite leaves with his concubine in tow. She does not appear to be consulted at all.

I wonder about that. Like, if she had the nerve to leave him in the first place, did she really just go back with him without objection? Did she say no, again, only to be ignored? Did she plead with her father to intervene, only to be told it was her duty to return? Had this whole escapade happened before, I wonder? They say it takes the average woman seven attempts to leave her abuser, but that is in today's world, where leaving is less difficult than it used to be. How many times did she try to communicate her truth, only to have it shut down?

And later, when he throws her out the door to be gang-raped while he saves his own neck? Did she protest then too? Was he able to ignore her in the hour of her great peril because he was so practiced at dismissing her wants?

The next morning, when he gets up—because somehow he was able to sleep—there at the entrance of the house she lies, interrupting his departure, and I wonder, *Why did she come back?* Surely not because she wanted *him* after all that had happened. Maybe she came back in order to leave a message, to force him to see what became of her. Maybe by choosing to breathe her last breath right where she knew she'd be blocking his pathway, she was still trying to speak.

When he opens the door and finds her there, he simply says, "Get up; let's go." These are the first words—and the only words—he speaks to her in this story. Remember how he went to his father-in-law's house to "speak to her heart," to convince her to come back? But this is all he ever says: "Get up; let's go." Lots of woo, that one. How did he get from wanting to win her back to being willing to hand her over to rapists and leave without her? Is it because he never truly valued her humanity to begin with? We already know he did not value or respect her truth.

When he tells her to get up, she makes no response. Without ceremony or any show of grief or remorse, he picks her up, takes her home, and chops up her body with a knife. He sends her pieces to the twelve tribes of Israel, after which people say, "Has such a thing ever happened since the day that the Israelites came up from the land of Egypt until this day? Consider it, take counsel, and speak out." The word *consider* is a translation of the Hebrew idiom "Direct to the heart," followed by "to her." In other words, they witness her mutilated body and say, "*Speak to her heart*, take counsel, and speak."

And for a brief moment, I feel this glimmer of hope that the nation will do what the husband failed to do—that even though her life is gone, they will still find a way to speak to her heart.

But my hopes are quickly dashed. Because this is how the tribes respond: With war and massacre. With a second massacre. With rape. With kidnapping. With more rape.

There is nothing left to do with this story but to write the next chapter ourselves. There is nothing left to do but to speak to her heart ourselves, since no one else would.

Do not run from this tale because it is uncomfortable and agonizing. Pledge to see the arenas in our own times where this narrative still plays out. You may think this story is far removed from our own, but it is not. When I think of her body chopped into pieces, I think of every victim of assault who has ever tried to tell what has happened to her and the way we tear her story to shreds, looking for holes. Truth-telling comes at a high cost, especially for women.

When I think of the concubine's husband cutting her up like that, as if she hasn't already been through enough, I think of the way survivors who come forward quickly are required to get rape kits for proof, which feels like being violated all over again. I think of how retelling the story can be as traumatizing as living it—and, bonus, when you tell it, there's often an audience to drive home your feelings of humiliation and to cast suspicion and doubt onto your reality. I think about the internet and how easy it is to chew someone up and spit them back out, how cyberbullying and trolling make the experience of telling your truth all the more excruciating because you can't talk about it without being abused. And if you stay quiet, they abuse you for that too. *Why didn't you speak up sooner?*

TRUTH-TELLING COMES AT A HIGH COST, ESPECIALLY FOR WOMEN.

When I think about her death, I think about how many victims never get to tell their own stories either because they don't live to tell it or because the media or the abuser or the family mistells the story for them. When I think about her failed attempt to leave her husband, I think about how hard it is to leave and stay away, even when you might be safer on your own. I think about how impossible it can be to really get away, to recover your own worth in a culture that refuses to acknowledge it. I think about how real her story is today in the twenty-first century, and I implore you, please, do not just walk away.

WE CAN LIVE IN A TIME WHEN SOME WOMEN HAVE MORE OPPORTUNITY THAN WOMEN HAVE EVER HAD BEFORE AND SOME WOMEN ARE BRUTALIZED AND TERRORIZED ON A DAILY BASIS. MOST WOMEN ARE CAUGHT SOMEWHERE IN BETWEEN. EVEN THE MOST SUCCESSFUL WOMEN ARE NOT SAFE FROM DANGER.

I think about the old man who graciously offers his home to the Levite and his concubine, not knowing the horror that is about to knock on his door. I think about how horrified he is when the men want to rape his male guest, how he begs them not to do it. How in desperation he offers them not just the Levite's concubine but *his own daughter* and how this must have felt horrible to him as a father. (In the end, only the concubine ends up outside the doors.) But I am so struck by this man's offer because he does it to save his guest, which means that it was *his sense of hospitality, not his perverseness,* that made him willing to sacrifice the women. He thought he was choosing a lesser evil—a moral logic that only works if the wider worldview says women are lesser and accepts it as fact. He is a good-hearted man caught in an evil system, making evil choices he thinks are good ones. I think about how many men I have known who are like this old man. They are kind and generous and hospitable and resistant to evildoers, but if it comes down to a choice between protecting the person with more power—that is, protecting his fellow man—or defending the marginalized woman, he will choose the preservation of the brotherhood over the dignity of women nearly every time. Feminists have a name for this brother. He is called the benevolent patriarchy. It is made up of the nice guys who think they care—and they do care until their own necks are on the line or their brother's neck is on the line, and then suddenly, the Good Old Boys Club matters more than justice, matters more than the woman or women right in front of their faces who are suffering.

I think about how Ruth and Naomi and Hannah were all contemporaries of this unnamed concubine wife—women who lived during the period of Judges and were seen and heard by God and by their communities. This tells me that horror and honor can coexist in the same place. We can live in a time when some women have more opportunity than women have ever had before *and* some women are brutalized and terrorized on a daily basis. Most women are caught somewhere in between. Even the most successful women are not safe from danger.

A couple of years ago, I was asked to speak about "a day in the life" of a female pastor. I chose a specific day, August 10, 2016. It was a day that still stood out in my memory and a day whose events I had recorded in my journal.

My memories of that day begin at lunch: I am eating with a congregant who thanks me for addressing sexual assault from the pulpit. I sense her comment is weighted, so I ask what the story is. Her niece, Kari, was murdered in 2006. Police ruled it a suicide because her husband, Matt, a Baptist pastor, said it was suicide. But my congregant pressed for an investigation. "How did you know it was murder?" I ask.

Well, she tells me, there was the time during his undergraduate degree when Matt attempted to assault a student. The university told police they would handle it, but then Matt was accepted as a student at the school's seminary. There was another assault while he was on staff at a local church; this time, the pastor in charge kept it quiet so as not to ruin Matt's reputation.

After lunch, I can't concentrate. I spend the afternoon googling "Matt Baker," reading about his eventual murder conviction and about the various accusations of sexual assault and harassment against him. I read a column in *Texas Monthly* from 2008 about the story, and some detail I read triggers my own experience with assault. PTSD means I relive my trauma as a present reality with every flashback. It's part of what makes the work difficult—women feel safe telling me their stories, so I pastor on the outside and hold down my trauma on the inside.

I am reading about Matt Baker in my church office like it's a compulsion when the custodian walks in. "Your haircut looks better than the one you had before," he says.

"Thank you?" I say, not sure how to respond.

"I would know," he adds with a smile. "I'm a connoisseur of women."

I freeze. I can't think, so I look away. A little later, I leave for a pastoral visit. On the way, I take a call from a friend. She went for a swim at her apartment today. Now she is distraught because she saw a man watching her from his balcony above the pool with his hand down his pants.

"I think you ought to report him," I say. Then I wonder if my custodian's remark was inappropriate. I can never seem to tell when it's directed at me. They say men take advantage of positions of power, but I am his boss. This isn't supposed to happen to me anymore, right?

The woman I am visiting for pastoral care is dying. She begins telling me about her cats, but before long, it's about her parents. She describes her mother as "complicit in the abuse."

I grimace slightly. "Did your dad . . . ?"

"Sexual abuse," she replies matter-of-factly. "He wasn't like that all the time," she adds to reassure me. I am not reassured.

I am on my way back to church for a meeting with the personnel committee. I have some proposals I want them to consider, but now I am nervous because I don't know whether to tell them about the custodian. (Why is this so hard?) I decide I will maybe, probably, tell them.

I am a competent preacher and pastor, but this has me feeling like a kid about to tattle. *Why do I feel so small?* The meeting starts. I feel my stomach lurch. I feel irrationally afraid. I speak quietly and begin. When I repeat the line "connoisseur of women," they laugh. But this is not funny to me. I pause. I almost lose my nerve. I finish the story. The only other woman in the room says, "That's harassment." I cringe. I don't want him to get in trouble on account of me.

Driving home, I think of Matt Baker, how he spent his ministry days as a sexual predator, how people trusted him. I think about scores of abused women no one believes. If I tell their stories, will people believe me? After all, I am a pastor. Then again, I am a woman, so I don't know.

As grotesque as the story about the concubine in Judges 19 is, I do not find her story so hard to relate to. The first time I preached about the concubine, it just so happened to be the same week of the Brett Kavanaugh hearings in which Christine Blasey Ford so bravely told her truth and then, as expected, had her testimony pulverized by the public. I hadn't picked the text about the concubine because it was relevant to the weekly news cycle; I had planned to preach that text months ago, and as it turned out, the ancient story was extremely relevant to current events. It is *still* so very hard for a woman to tell the truth; for a woman to feel safe; for a woman to experience the men in her life as trustworthy; for a woman to make it through this life with body, heart, and mind intact; for a woman to escape abuse without being followed; for a woman to believe the systems that are meant to protect her will, in fact, protect her; for a woman to expect justice; for a woman to be seen as anything more than a pawn of the patriarchy; for a woman to know she is not expendable.

I propose we take up where the Levite and the tribes of Israel so clearly failed. It is well past time that we speak to her heart.

Speak to her heart in this way: believe her. I believe that in the queendom, truth-telling will be the norm rather than the exception, but if you want to *be* more of a truth-teller, that means you have to increase your capacity for hearing the truth first. So when a woman tells you her truth, listen. Understand it is not your job to cross-examine. Believe her. I'm not saying that if you are on a jury in a courtroom, you should ignore any evidence against her. I'm saying if she comes to you in private looking for a confidante, believe her. I'm saying if you hear her testimony secondhand or in the public forum,

> IT IS STILL *SO VERY HARD FOR A WOMAN TO TELL THE TRUTH, FOR A WOMAN TO FEEL SAFE, FOR A WOMAN TO EXPERIENCE THE MEN IN HER LIFE AS TRUSTWORTHY, FOR A WOMAN TO MAKE IT THROUGH THIS LIFE WITH BODY, HEART, AND MIND INTACT.*

believe her. At the very least, don't blame her, don't shame her, don't chop her to pieces. If you have your doubts, at the very least, don't say them out loud. Because *even if* she is one of the

2 to 7 percent who are false accusers, what you say about her will be overheard by other survivors, and they will hear your doubt of her as doubt of them, and they will take note that you are not safe to tell their stories to. They will hear your doubt of her, and for some, it will trigger long-standing PTSD symptoms. You won't know it, but your comment will be what sends her to the therapist's office this week—that is, if she's lucky and can afford a therapist, if she was able to find a good one, if she didn't choose an easier but more destructive form of coping instead.

Speak to her heart. Speak to her heart by listening. God has not called you to be a commentator on other people's trauma. Speak to her heart by seeing that she has one and knowing that it bleeds. It is not your story to cut up and dissect. Her story is not for your entertainment. She is not an intellectual exercise. She is not your **WHEN A WOMAN TELLS YOU HER TRUTH, LISTEN.** debate topic or your dinner gossip; she is a person. You are not the expert on her life, on what she should or could have done or should or could do now. You will never be the expert. It is her story and her life; she is the expert.

Speak to her heart. Speak to her heart by respecting and honoring her pain. Do not call her emotional or extreme or irrational or hysterical or over the top. Tell her she is a sane person dealing with insane circumstances.

Speak to her heart by abandoning benevolent patriarchy and the security it affords you.

Speak to her heart by refusing to excuse violence. Do not say "Boys will be boys." Look, I get it that our culture sends all sorts of wrong messages to boys about what it means to be a man and how to pursue a woman and not take no for an answer. It is hard work to get beyond the cultural messaging and find a different way to be. It terrifies me to think about raising boys because it's actually *not* easy to teach them not to rape. The culture does not honor consent or make it sexy. No matter what you try to teach your children, there is a whole culture out there counterteaching them, and the culture is more powerful than your parenting and that is terrifying. It's hard work, and we have to recognize what we're up against. But just because society encourages rape and promotes coercion, that doesn't make men not guilty. What it means is that patriarchy and rape culture are real and pervasive and invasive, and it's not just that it could or might affect you. It has affected you. Rape culture and patriarchal thinking are embedded in your psyche; they are the air you breathe when you wake up in the morning, and if you can't see that, that poison will stay inside you, harming you and others until the day you die.

Speak to her heart by making a lifetime commitment—because it will take a lifetime—to confront the sexism that lives and breathes in you. The best chance your children and grand-children have of overcoming the toxicity of sexism is to see the ongoing work of liberation practiced and modeled in you as you set yourself free one revelation, one choice, one repentance at a time.

BUT JUST BECAUSE THE CULTURE ENCOURAGES RAPE AND PROMOTES COERCION, THAT DOESN'T MAKE MEN NOT GUILTY.

Speak to her heart by telling the truth about sexism as you encounter it alive and well in yourself and in the wider culture. Do not leave her the burden of telling the truth all by herself.

The truth is a powerful, powerful force—one that keeps on resurrecting no matter how many times it is crucified. Kind of like Christ. Kind of like women. Even the concubine, who never got her life or limbs back, has a story we can keep resurrecting. May we speak truth to power, speak truth to her heart, speak truth with our sisters, and rise.

CHAPTER 6

I Want to See You Be Brave

We were walking by a pond when my two-year-old daughter saw some geese up ahead and started moving toward them with her arms stretched wide.

"What are you doing, Leila?" I asked.

"Hold geese!" she said affectionately.

Before I knew it, the geese started heading toward us. Leila's demeanor changed. She looked scared. But she straightened herself up to two-and-a-half feet tall, pointed her finger at the pond, and shouted, "Go! Go back to water, geese!"

I so admire a woman who knows it is okay to change her mind and to say it out loud when she does.

One of the scariest parts about being a writer is that my thoughts are out there in the world for other people to read. I mean, I recognize that is sort of *the point* of being a writer. But I know myself, and I know I evolve, and I know that someday, I will look back on things I have written today and no longer entirely agree with myself. I will have changed my mind. I will have grown. I will think differently, feel differently, understand differently.

The knowledge that what I write today may no longer seem adequate in the future can be paralyzing. Why write if it isn't right? I would say that I have learned not to let the fear of failure stop me from taking action, but that's not quite right. It isn't so much a fear of failure that holds me back as it is a *fear of growth*. Getting it wrong but not knowing you're wrong can be a kind of bliss. Ignorant bliss, but still, largely painless. But discovering new information that invites change can be so uncomfortable. How many times do we stunt our own growth because we don't want to admit that what we're doing needs a course correction?

There is nothing, absolutely nothing, wrong with changing your mind. Sometimes the old snakeskin simply doesn't fit anymore, and you're not serving anyone by staying crammed inside. We act like it is embarrassing if we quit a job we thought we wanted, leave a relationship we used to think would last forever, change a belief we once held dear—but isn't it worse to hold on to something we now know isn't working? So what if it used to work? Or if we used to think it worked? We are responsible for what we do with what we know *now*. What we did *before* we knew better can now be forgiven. What we *don't do* with our knowing (now that we know) can really mess us up.

THERE IS NOTHING, ABSOLUTELY NOTHING, WRONG WITH CHANGING YOUR MIND.

In the queendom, we don't just tell the truth; we live it. Once we know, we act. And we don't avoid knowing, even if knowing will lead to some painful course correction. As new information comes in, we adapt, and we adapt without apology. We tell those geese to go back into the pond when hugging them is no longer a good idea.

If you are going to be the type of person who explores her full landscape and doesn't stay put inside the confines of the kingdom, you are bound to learn new information, to discover new territory, and to gain unforeseen insights. Discovery makes demands of you and requires you to do something about that which you have found, to honor the riches of what you have unearthed. Many people opt to stay put because remaining where you are is less taxing. Sure, staying put requires your conformity, but it doesn't require your original, unscripted response as the unknown gradually makes itself known, which is a much wilder venture.

While it may feel way scarier, it is a mistake, I believe, to assert that engaging the unknown is inherently more dangerous than remaining in the known. Are there dangers to stepping out into the new and unknown, where you might find it necessary to change your mind or change your perceptions? Yes. But the dangers of staying put can be far more toxic.

I think about Jephthah in Judges 11. He is the epitome of refusing to change one's mind. Here is a man who, in order to win a battle, pledges to the Lord that *if* he wins, he will sacrifice to God whatever walks out of his home first upon his return. It is important to note that this is a vow Jephthah comes up with on his own, not something God asks of him. It is also worth noting that the spirit of God comes upon Jephthah *before* he makes this absurd vow. In other words, God is already with him. A vow isn't necessary.

Lo and behold, the first "thing" out of his door when he returns home from victory is not a fatted calf ready for sacrifice but his daughter, his only child, running out to greet him. I'm not sure how he didn't anticipate this happening, but he acts shocked and grieved. He says to her, "I am devastated. I have made a vow to the Lord that I cannot break," referring to the fact that he now has to kill her—only, he doesn't explain why he can't break the vow. Presumably something to do with his own sense of honor?

I often imagine the mother of this young girl assigned to slaughter, even though the text leaves her out of the story entirely. I imagine the mother begging her husband to reconsider, to break his vow for the sake of love, to preserve their daughter's life at all costs. I also imagine her praying, begging God to intervene. Like the ram for Isaac, she begs for a ram to spare her daughter.

Only there is no ram. *Or, at least, Jephthah doesn't notice one.* Maybe there are a dozen rams on his way to sacrifice his daughter, but he pays them no heed. He isn't open to new information. He certainly doesn't pay attention to his wife or anyone else who might have tried to tell him this was a bad idea and not at all the kind of thing God would want. He sets his path and will not deviate. I do not think it is faithfulness that inspires him. I think he is afraid of learning he has made a mistake, and so in the end, he kills her. He would rather follow through on his first impulse and hug the geese than change course, even if his internal alarm bells are going off. I am reminded of a father I know who is so utterly convinced that being gay is wrong that he will not listen to any new information about the topic at all, even though his current theology is asking him to sacrifice his relationship with his gay daughter.

Jephthah's story is the rigidity of patriarchy at its worst. There is no flow, no adaptation, no listening to the nature of the land. It's like discovering a mountain in your path, but instead of forging a natural path around it, you blow the whole thing up with dynamite and disrespect the guidance the landscape is trying to offer you. You dominate the information rather than learning from it, you bully your way ahead instead of stopping to listen, *you assume it is more dangerous to change than it is to stay steadfast.* It is arrogance that conflates stubbornness with faithfulness and confuses fidelity to sameness with fidelity to God. It is the kind of religion that produces senseless violence and calls it faith.

In truth, all choices have consequences. The question is, Which consequences am I prepared to live with? The consequences of wrongheaded fidelity can be fatal. Bravery also has consequences, but while bravery will cost you, it will also give back to you. Bravery will give you things such as your own integrity, the feeling of being alive, the satisfaction that you did something. In Jephthah's case, the bravery to break his vow would have given him his daughter back.

Earlier in Judges, there is another story of violence, but this time the assassin is a woman. Her name is Jael, and she is a foreigner (non-Israelite). The Israelites are at war with the Canaanites, who have been oppressing them. Sisera is the commander of the Canaanite army, and the Israelites are able to defeat all his troops. Sisera flees to the tent of Jael, whose family is friendly with the Canaanites. He expects safety and hospitality, and Jael offers him a place to lie down and rest. Only, while he is sleeping, she takes a tent stake and drives it into his head.

WHILE BRAVERY WILL COST YOU, IT WILL ALSO GIVE BACK TO YOU.

It is exceedingly rare in Scripture that we hear of a woman killing anyone, and I am fascinated by her. While the story is indeed grotesque, I find it curious that while I had to discover Jael on my own by reading the Bible as a teenager, I learned about David and Goliath over and over from a very young age, even though David kills Goliath first with a sling, then takes Goliath's sword and chops off his head.

I once heard a group of clergywomen say we can't look to Jael as a hero because she uses violence. Maybe that is true. At the very least, however, if we're going to get uncomfortable around a woman who uses violence, then we have to stop admiring men who've used violence: King David, Hercules,

George Washington, Davy Crockett, Bruce Lee, Nelson Mandela, the Hulk—all of 'em. (Some of these men/characters may be more worthy of admiration than others, but the point is, they all used violence.)

It's not like this woman set out to kill an army commander. But he showed up unexpectedly in her life, and she knew this unexpected event *required* something of her. Decorum would have said this event—the arrival of her husband's friend—required her hospitality. Typical expectations of women would have said this event required her domesticity.

IF WE'RE GOING TO GET UNCOMFORTABLE AROUND A WOMAN WHO USES VIOLENCE, THEN WE HAVE TO STOP ADMIRING MEN WHO'VE USED VIOLENCE.

But wartime required something else from her. It was of no personal advantage to her to kill Sisera, for her family was on good terms with the Canaanites, yet she took it upon herself to slay him anyway. (The person who defeated Goliath, on the other hand, was promised the king's daughter, great wealth, and an exemption from all taxes. Jael, unlike David, had nothing to gain.) The text doesn't tell us her motive, so we are left wondering if she'd seen the oppression of her neighbors at the hands of the Canaanites and decided enough was enough.

With the army general at her doorstep (i.e., tent flap), Jael *had to* make a call. Initially, she went out to meet him and invited him in, as expected. He asked for water; she gave him milk and covered him with a blanket. It was as if she was mothering him, which makes me so curious as to *when* she decided to kill him. Was it when she first saw him? Was she luring him in with her nurturing assurances? Or was she simply doing what was expected of her as a woman until suddenly, it dawned on her that the man lying asleep at her feet had oppressed the Israelites and abandoned his troops and was now at her mercy? Commentators often treat Jael as if she was conniving all along—creating a false sense of security to entice Sisera into the tent to sleep—but I am skeptical of that interpretation. She couldn't possibly have known he was going to show up, so my instinct is to assume that her initial response to him was automatic. Presumably, she knew how to play the hostess. That was familiar and regular, like second nature. Slaying an army general? Totally out of the question before now. I think she made a pivot midhostessing.

Was it the right call to slaughter him? It was such a violent choice, and it's really hard for me to say what was right thousands of years removed from the situation. But based on the information we have, I know that her decision took guts and that it was brave and risky. By eliminating the leader of the Canaanite army, Jael helped set the Hebrew people free from their oppressors. Jephthah's act of violence, on the other hand, helped no one.

It is worth noting that Jephthah's personal story begins as that of an outcast. He is an illegitimate child who was cast out of Gilead at a young age by his brothers, who did not want any of their inheritance going to "the son of another woman." The archetype of an outcast is an important one, and most of us can identify with it in some form. Maybe we were literally rejected by family, or maybe we felt rejected at school or at church, cast aside by the "cool kids" or by the "smart kids" or by whomever. Maybe we've felt boxed out at work or like we've never been anyone's favorite. It's not hard to imagine the pain of Jephthah's early life.

Much later, when the people of Gilead are in trouble, to Jephthah's surprise, they turn to him for help. Imagine: the rejected one now asked to be the hero. It isn't just the fate of the people resting on this victory—Jephthah's own legitimacy is at stake. Win the battle, and for the first time, he could really be one of them. You can perhaps see why this victory is so crucial for Jephthah, why he cares so much. He doesn't just *want* to win; he *needs* to win. He has something to prove. He has a deep childhood wound that craves resolution. And so Jephthah attempts to bargain with God. God, as we've already noted, does not even show up for that conversation because no such bargaining is necessary.

When we encounter the outcast archetype in literature, the story is asking us to go within and identify the outcast inside ourselves. It asks us to notice what parts of ourselves we have cast out or cast aside. The tighter we've drawn the boundaries of our inner kingdom, the more pieces of ourselves lurk in the shadows, outside the circle of belonging—not welcome, not included in our decisions. In order to feel like we belong, we ignore the parts of ourselves that don't fit a kingdom mold, and in doing so, we cast out essential wisdom. Jephthah, it seems, is so intent on belonging, on finding his place in the system, that he casts aside his own fatherhood. Instead of healing the wounds inside himself, he projects them outward, onto God. He seems to believe that if he doesn't keep his vow, God will reject him, though God has said no such thing. He wants God to see him as legitimate too—maybe by doing the extraordinary, he can finally earn his place in the kingdom. By rejecting the voice of his inner wisdom nudging him to change course, he ultimately rejects his own daughter—so much so that he kills her. In sacrificing his daughter, he sacrifices his best self;

> **THE TIGHTER WE'VE DRAWN THE BOUNDARIES OF OUR INNER KINGDOM, THE MORE PIECES OF OURSELVES LURK IN THE SHADOWS, OUTSIDE THE CIRCLE OF BELONGING—NOT WELCOME, NOT INCLUDED IN OUR DECISIONS.**

in sacrificing his best self, he sacrifices his daughter. How many children end up wounded by a parent who refuses to do their inner work, who refuses to change and to choose their best self?

It is critical that we be brave, not just because the world needs our courage, but because the healing of our souls and our families require it. If we're not brave enough to find what is wounded in us and begin the difficult journey of bringing our scattered parts back together, we will inadvertently contribute to the fragmentation of the world around us, not to mention the continuing disintegration of the self. This means truth-telling cannot be limited to telling the truth about what has happened to us. We must also find ways to tell the truth about what is happening *inside* us.

> **IT IS CRITICAL THAT WE BE BRAVE, NOT JUST BECAUSE THE WORLD NEEDS OUR COURAGE, BUT BECAUSE THE HEALING OF OUR SOULS AND OUR FAMILIES REQUIRE IT.**

Author, priest, and contemplative Alan Jones writes, "The saint who thinks he casts no shadow is very dangerous." By denying the role that his childhood wound played in his actions, I believe Jephthah's pain came out sideways, resulting in the death of his daughter, a murder that Jephthah ironically carried out in fidelity to his unexamined sense of self-righteousness.

I would argue that Jael's impulse to stop the evil general did not arise from her unexamined shadow. Many women have buried the impulse toward aggression and self-protection so deep, they cannot access it all. The fact that she was *able* to act decisively implies that she had, on some level, integrated her maternal, mama-bear instinct to protect the vulnerable and the oppressed, and she had, on some level, integrated her animus energy that prompted her to act. Whereas Jephthah's unintegrated shadow leads him to be violent toward the innocent, Jael's more fully integrated shadow leads her to defend the innocent, even though her act of defense utilized violence.

Suppressed and unexamined internal violence is likely to find expression externally in potentially catastrophic ways. For example, a gentle pacifist by the name of Henry Winter, who lived during World War II and was a caring country doctor, became infatuated by a woman who rejected him. To the shock of all who knew him, he retaliated against her by shooting her and then killing himself. His friend John Mortimer wrote this about the horrible incident: "I think about these things often, but cannot explain them. I can only suggest that Henry Winter suffered terribly and unusually from having rejected the violence which was made available to us all at the age when we went to Oxford."

Perhaps Jephthah's acts of violence were the external results of an internal conflict he never resolved—that is, his inward experience of feeling the outcast. If he had done his inner work to accept himself despite his family's rejection (i.e., if he had discontinued the violence being done to him by giving himself love and acceptance), perhaps he could also have accepted himself as one who breaks his own vow when the morality of the promise becomes untenable.

By contrast, I wonder if Jael's external act of violence was tied to an inward act of liberation. Had she merely showed hospitality to the evil general as was expected of her and restrained herself from intervening in Israel's deliverance, she would have been enacting a *different kind of violence*—a violence toward herself, a violation of her own sense of integrity and self-respect, a disregard for that nudging within to act in defense of the Hebrew people.

At the heart of bravery is the willingness to allow that which is repressed and hiding in the shadows out into the light of day, and then to allow that new knowledge to shape and mold us, even if it significantly alters our course.

Some of the ways our repressed material comes to light are through our dreams, through myth, through art. Images and stories have a way of penetrating the defenses of the conscious mind. For example, dreams may tell wild stories, but the stories never lie. When our conscious mind goes to sleep, the unconscious speaks to us, telling us what our conscious mind is perhaps fearful to acknowledge. Dreams are one of the ways the queendom calls to us long before our waking self has taken its first step outside the kingdom. (I wonder what Jael had been dreaming about those nights before Sisera showed up at her door, don't you?)

I think of a particularly powerful dream in my own life that eventually propelled me further into my own queendom territory. But first I had to grapple with the dream's violence, allowing the surprisingly murderous components of my psyche into the light for examination.

In my dream, a high school star football player contracted a rare and debilitating disease that was slowly eating away at his muscular function. It was getting so bad that the athlete could barely even run anymore. In the dream, the boy is in his backyard with his girlfriend, who is cheering him on as he tries desperately to run again. He starts to run, but his legs won't cooperate, and before you know it, he is tripping over himself, smacking his face into a chain-link fence as he tumbles to the ground. The girlfriend emits a loud sob as he falls, and slowly he picks himself up and stumbles his way back across the yard to his grieving girlfriend. He reaches out his arms to her as if to comfort her, and she falls into him, but then she slumps suddenly to the ground, and I realize she is dead. He has stabbed her with a knife and killed her.

I woke up from this dream and thought to myself, *What the heck is wrong with my brain that I dreamt up that disturbing story?* But I'd been learning about dreams and how they carry messages for us from the unconscious, and although I could not fathom what sort of message my graphic homicidal dream could possibly have for sweet little innocent me, I asked a mentor for help interpreting it. I felt embarrassed to relay my violent nightmare, but he was excited. "Disturbing dreams are the best kind!" he said. I felt skeptical, but we began to work the dream anyway.

By the end of our conversation, my mind was teeming with real-life connections. For me, the teenage football player represented the arenas where I have been successful in life so far, but something was happening to my soul, and I couldn't keep living my old life. All the effort to keep doing my same old stuff made me feel like I was being eaten alive.

In other words, I knew I needed to quit my job. At first, this was terrifying, and I tried to will myself to be the old me, but when I tried, I ran into a fence, a barrier. My soul was saying, "No more."

The girlfriend in the dream represented that part of me that was grieving this loss and could not accept what was happening. She needed me to be a star athlete. But the athlete in me took a very decisive, though unexpected, action. The athlete decided this girlfriend energy needed to die—that is, the part of me that was pushing me to stay the same and succeed in the same ways as always—that part needed to quiet down in order to let something new emerge.

The atrophy of my muscles wasn't so much a curse as it was a push in a new direction; it was a warning bell that I couldn't keep pushing myself in the same ways and get the same results. But if I listened to the girlfriend, the atrophy was all bad with no good to be had. And so I had to shut her up. As it turns out, the violence in my dream wasn't so violent—it was a metaphor about stopping the side of me that was doing violence to myself by forcing me to stay the same. The girlfriend in the dream appeared to be supportive, but in reality, she was keeping the boy from listening to his body, accepting his new fate, and learning a new way to be himself in the world.

The appearance of violence in our dreams isn't always a bad thing. The dream violence may represent a boundary we need to set in waking life, for example. Or if the violence is being done *to* us in the dream, the dream may be trying to reveal to us some way in which we are being violated or doing harm to ourselves.

That being said, as I continue to evolve, I wonder if a more compassionate response to the girlfriend in my dream might work just as well or even better. I am now considering how she might be integrated into the narrative rather than eliminated. How might I take her feelings seriously without allowing her demands to run the show? Just because my dream presented me with the information that her energy was hurting me doesn't mean I have to respond to her with violence. I could choose to break up with her, for example—without, you know, murdering her. I could sit down and have a negotiation with her about what the future me needs. I could invite her along with me on the journey to becoming something new. I could find her a therapist. I could tell her I've used up too much energy placating and comforting her, and she needs to leave me alone now. I could ask her to hold us a grief ritual for saying goodbye to my football-athlete self, then afterward, we could eat ice cream and brainstorm what we want to accomplish together outside the stadium walls.

Instead of either suppressing or letting loose our violent inclinations, what if we were playful with them? Personified them in our imaginations? Talked to them, found out what they needed from us?

From a metaphorical standpoint, the initial violence in my dream helped me get beyond my hurdles to do what needed to be done. The violence was movement forward. If I hadn't acted, I would have remained stuck in an unhealthy pattern. And yet, I don't have to stay with my initial violent response either. I can evolve beyond that as well. *I can keep changing.*

One of my favorite, most overlooked characteristics of God in the Bible is that *God changes*. For example, in Exodus 32, God is absolutely furious with the people for building a golden calf—so furious, God becomes intent on destroying them, but Moses intervenes on the people's behalf. The text says, "The Lord relented and did not bring on his people the disaster he had threatened." Or, depending on your translation, God changed God's mind, or God repented. Repentance simply means to change direction, and in the Bible, *even God repents.*

And look, if even God can change, then you and I sure as hell don't need to be running around like stubborn little Jephthahs, afraid to alter our course. We can take a good, solid look deep within to see what is causing us to stay the same. If needed, we can choose a different motivation. Or maybe the motivation itself makes sense, but the resulting actions don't match our values, and we need to consider new options. For example, if I'm right that Jephthah's whole ridiculous vow stemmed from his deep need to belong, what if he had examined that need but thought about how else he might feed it? Instead of making and keeping foolhardy promises in an attempt to secure victory in war . . . what if he had decided to embrace the belonging that *was already his*—that is, the love of his daughter, rushing out the door to greet him? How might the recognition of their mutual belonging to each other have stopped him in his tracks and caused him to change course?

I don't mean to equate bravery with changing course. Sometimes it takes just as much courage to stand your ground. What I do mean to suggest is that bravery is rarely static. Even when you are staying put—sticking it out through a tough situation with your kid, staying in a difficult job because you know you can make a difference, working on a relationship after trust has been broken, and so on—even the staying requires adaptation. Sometimes bravery looks like staying rooted in one place while adjusting to the changes that are happening around you and to you. But whether you go or stay, there's no doubt about it: one of the hallmarks of a queendom citizen is courage. This way of life requires participation. There can be no bystanders.

When Sisera shows up at Jael's place, she doesn't just do what is expected of her. She is willing to ask herself how she wants to show up to the moment, and then she dreams up previously unimagined responses.

I find it striking that in the first part of Jephthah's story, in the short span of twenty-six verses, Jephthah asks *nine* questions. But after he makes his vow? There are no more questions. Only statements. It's like he stopped questioning. Maybe a single question could have altered everything.

If you don't have a damn clue how to start being brave because you've been careful for far too long, start by asking questions. Just like a dream, a good question opens you to possibilities you had yet to consider. My daughter Leila isn't afraid to question anything. Maybe that's common for a two-year-old, but it's also one of the reasons she's my hero.

CHAPTER 7

Not Your Cross to Bear

When meditating in the past, I would visualize a giant, flat rock. The rock was sitting motionless in a gushing river, and I would imagine myself sitting serenely on the rock while my thoughts rushed by me on the water. I would practice staying put and not diving in after my thoughts, allowing them to flow on past.

If letting my thoughts swim by became too hard, I'd add a waterfall. Because, I reasoned, if my thoughts went over the falls, I definitely wouldn't be able to retrieve them. The thoughts were long gone. I had to surrender them. At least, that is what I tried to convince myself by imagining them falling, falling away from me.

Perhaps not surprisingly, my thoughts weren't too compliant, and somehow they would find me again, usually right away. Before they'd even fully disappeared over the ledge, there they were, spraying me with their mist, determined to cling to me. The visualization started to give me anxiety. The falls weren't succeeding at thought removal, and if I was honest, I didn't actually want my thoughts to leave me so soon.

When I saw Niagara Falls for the first time in real life, I couldn't stop staring. It was like looking at the body of a goddess; I was mesmerized. I was mesmerized not only by the falling water but by the river itself before it reached the falls. There was so much turbulence on the surface—huge rapids that looked as if the water was struggling with itself. If you focused on only one small area of rapids, you couldn't even tell which way the river was flowing because, on the surface, the water crashed into itself and sprayed up into the air, like a great contest for direction. But of course, I knew that was only how things appeared on the surface and from a limited view. If you sunk beneath the colliding waves, the river was only flowing in one direction, and it was traveling with force.

I've changed my meditation visualization. The river is still there, and the water still contains my thoughts as well as my feelings, but I am no longer sitting on a rock above the water. Instead, I sink down, down, down to the lowest level of rushing water. I am no longer trying to sit still in this meditation. I am letting the flow of my life carry me. By sinking down, I can look up at my thoughts and feelings that are in tumult up above me. I notice them, they are a part of me, and I experience their battle. But my truest self dwells deeper than the turbulence. When this deep part of me hits a large rock or an obstacle of some kind, I glide around it as the force of the river guides me. Without even trying, I shift as necessary to remain in the flow. I have no need to move the rock because I am water. Deep water. Deep river water. I am not stationary rock. I am movement.

BUT MY TRUEST SELF DWELLS DEEPER THAN THE TURBULENCE.

I made the mistake in earlier meditation practices of imagining my true self as *different and distinct from* my thoughts and feelings, as if I could separate myself from them and stay on the surface of things. The problem with this was that I stayed on the surface of things. I didn't explore myself from a place of deep knowing and truth. I detached from myself and learned how to feel peace-by-suppression.

When I began to accept that my thoughts and feelings *are* me but not the whole of me, I connected with myself in a deeper way and occasionally even felt peace-by-acceptance, though acceptance usually came long after contact with the rapids of grief and anger and pain. I had to go through the turbulence and eventually sink below it. There is no such thing as simply watching my feelings and thoughts flow past *unless* I'm willing to lose my identity as river. My new understanding of meditation and self-awareness is to see myself as all that I think and feel, accepting the whole of it without rejection, and simultaneously to see myself as *more than* any singular thought or feeling that arises in a given moment.

Acceptance, by the way, doesn't mean you don't *do* anything about what is happening to you. Rather, acceptance is the precursor to taking appropriate action. If I don't accept that there is a big boulder in my way, I can't begin the work of making my way around it. I just keep slamming into it, pretending it isn't there, remaining stuck and unable to move forward. There is a certain peace that comes with acknowledging the boulder's existence because even if the boulder does mean changing course, at least I get to stop running into it as if it's not there, then wondering why I've got such a splitting headache all the time. The acceptance happens when I go deeper. Staying on the surface is like one never-ending crash.

Acceptance doesn't mean the feelings disappear over the falls and leave you alone. In fact, when you practice acceptance, you'll probably feel more instead of less because you're no longer ignoring or suppressing; you're allowing. This is good. Feelings, after all, are bearers of information. They don't just show up for the sheer flamboyance of expression; they show up waving flags that point the way forward or deeper. Feelings are a type of intelligence; it is the patriarchy that has convinced us they are stupid or an impractical nuisance. The patriarchy will tell you to separate feelings from rational thinking, so the one (emotion) can't taint the other (thinking). Wisdom integrates both. Patriarchy supports the split self, the compartmentalized self. Wisdom flows from the whole body of intelligence. This is why, when I meditate now, I no longer imagine that I am sitting above the water. I imagine that I am in the water, that I *am* the water. As water, I embrace everything in my flow.

FEELINGS ARE A TYPE OF INTELLIGENCE; IT IS THE PATRIARCHY THAT HAS CONVINCED US THEY ARE STUPID OR AN IMPRACTICAL NUISANCE.

One of the stories I find most compelling in the whole Bible—and you are going to think this is weird—is the one of Jephthah's daughter in Judges 11, that horrific tale of child sacrifice I discussed in the previous chapter. I know it's an awful, tragic story. I know it is a narrative full of injustice and that it is yet another account of violence against a woman. That is not why I love it. I love it for what I see when I dive deep, when I view this courageous girl from the vantage point of the depths. Let me tell you what I see.

Once she knows she is going to be killed, she says this to her father: "Grant me this one request. . . . Give me two months to roam the hills and weep with my friends, because I will never marry." In other words, "I'm taking some time for myself, since my life is being cut short, and you will let me have it." And she does it. She gathers her friends, roams the hills for two months, and mourns. I see *so much* in those two months:

1. She accepts her own death. I'm not saying women should put up with abuse or consent to the violence done to them. I'm just observing that *in this instance*, in which Jephthah's daughter probably had no other choice, she took the reality in front of her and made what she could out of it. She faces it head-on rather than head-down.

    IF SHE MUST GO DOWN, SHE IS GOING TO SET HER OWN TERMS. WITHIN THE CONFINES OF HER IMPRISONMENT, SHE STILL FINDS AGENCY.

    Of course, I prefer stories in which the women make it out alive, and we should keep telling those make-it-out-alive stories to one another because we need them. It's just that there is something so very real about the stories in which a woman doesn't make it because we've all known the story of a woman who doesn't survive. Remarkably, this young woman is able to face her impending death honestly. She's not in denial. She decides what to do with the time she has left. What I *like* about her story is that she decides if she must go down, she is going to set her own terms. Within the confines of her imprisonment, she still finds agency.

2. She does the unexpected. Where did a young girl—a child—come up with the idea to take time and space for herself? It's not like there is a road map for how to navigate your remaining days when your father is about to sacrifice you. This kid is creative. She thinks on her feet, she speaks up on her own behalf, and she comes up with something *she* wants. Her two months spent roaming the hills will not serve her father in any way because her request is not about him. It is about *her* and

her needs. She is a girl about to be sacrificed on account of her father's ego, and she has the wherewithal to think for herself and to innovate on the spot. And she does not just ask for her two months like someone hoping for a favor; she insists on it like she deserves it.

3. She sets a boundary by demanding time and space for herself. Far too often, Christianity gives women the wrong idea about sacrifice. I realize it might seem a little odd to use the story of a girl who gets sacrificed as an example of someone with boundaries, but here is what I mean: she doesn't give up what is within her reach to keep. The system betrays her, but she refuses to betray herself. Sometimes this is the most we can do as women. The system may rob from us, but we keep what we can. That sounds discouraging, but I think that in dire times, these small acts of resistance are where the revolution remains alive—when women keep hold of the pieces of themselves that they can. There is a whole lot she cannot control in this story. She cannot stop her own demise. She cannot escape. But she does what is within her reach to do. She has the self-determination to shape her own ending. She demands more time. She keeps the perpetrator out of her life and out of her head while she can. Jephthah's daughter doesn't win the fight for her life, but that doesn't stop her from protecting what she can.

4. She creates space for her grief. She doesn't try to deny or suppress the horror of her own tragedy. She doesn't just allow herself to grieve; she deliberately sets aside time and space for her grief to billow and breathe. She invites others to bear witness. She doesn't use her remaining days doing anything but caring for herself and giving herself what she needs. She doesn't spend her remaining days

with family. Family is where her abuser comes from. She gathers around her chosen family who can fully see and honor her grief with her, who won't make the tragedy/ murder about them, as her father has. She does not cast her grief aside. And whereas her father was cast out by his family, **THE SYSTEM** then did everything in his **BETRAYS HER, BUT** power to earn back their favor, **SHE REFUSES TO** I think she recognizes his love **BETRAY HERSELF.** will never be hers and creates **SOMETIMES THIS IS** further distance between this **THE MOST WE CAN** false notion of love and herself. **DO AS WOMEN.** In so doing, she chooses a kind of two-month exile for herself—the kind of exile that will place her in kinship with women who can truly care for her in her hour of distress.

5.   She bands together with a sisterhood. She calls allies and sister-mourners to herself to roam the hills *with her*. She does not walk alone. I like to imagine what they did out there for two months in the hills on their own, no chaperone. The Scriptures don't tell us what happened because no one knows. What happened between those young women is secret, special, and sacred. There is nothing quite like the community that is born from tragedy and adversity.

   This sisterhood continues well beyond her dying breath. The text reports, "From this comes the Israelite tradition that each year the young women of Israel go out for four days to commemorate the daughter of Jephthah the Gileadite." Biblical scholar Phyllis Trible's translation of the verse says that despite her shortened life, "nevertheless she became a tradition." She probably had no idea she was starting a tradition, that she would be remembered in this ritualistic way by the sisterhood for years to come. When women come together to feel and to lament and to pay their respects, the effects ripple on for generations to come. There is an old Jewish legend about her that says every year on the anniversary of her death, water turns to blood, as if the very earth, the rivers and creeks, have not stopped mourning.

6. She *roams*. She leaves the "kingdom" behind while she can and takes to the hills. She explores nature, the land, her own grief, her approaching death. She doesn't stick to the familiar. She moves beyond her father's property lines, and she roams.

I am in awe of her. I mean, it sucks because she dies, but gosh darn it, she is fierce and wise for a young girl living in a male-dominated world that is literally out to kill her.

Of course, it is certainly appropriate to wonder whether she really had to die. Couldn't the village have risen up in her defense? Stood between her and danger? Thrown Jephthah in prison? Could she have run away? Fought back? There are other ways this story could have ended, some of them much more satisfactory. We have no way of knowing what else could have happened had various characters in the story (and characters not mentioned) chosen different responses. I'd like to think that had better resources been available to her, Jephthah's daughter would have survived. Then again, that thought makes me angry because *why weren't better resources available to her*? Why are some people afforded more agency while others seem to be born at the wrong place in the wrong time? Given that she does indeed die, it is important to remember that none of the evil done to her was her fault. A child cannot be expected to defend herself against her father. It is *his* job to protect *her*. Her protector and her killer are one and the same. How could she have possibly known what to do? Interestingly, in some midrashic retellings of this story by the ancient rabbis, she argues with her father about his plans to sacrifice her. The rabbis paint her as articulate in matters concerning the law, whereas Jephthah appears ignorant, but despite her best efforts, she does not persuade him.

Though she could not escape death, she took what she could and demanded two months for herself. Based on the limited options available to her, I think she was pretty strategic, self-defined, deliberate, and boundaried. As women, we are taught to observe external boundaries but not to create them for ourselves. We must stay within bounds, even if staying hurts us, and we must not draw any lines of our own. As a result, women are

IN THE QUEENDOM, BOUNDARIES LOOK LESS LIKE FENCES OR CAGES AND MORE LIKE SKIN.

constantly climbing onto crosses no one is forcing them to be on. Jephthah's daughter faced a terrible cross she couldn't prevent: murder. But there were other crosses she refused to carry: She wasn't going to play the role of comforting her father, her abuser, for example. She wasn't going to accept the journey to death without making some demands of her own. She wasn't going to "bear it alone," as if suffering silently is somehow more admirable than suffering in community.

In the queendom, each self gets to be boundaried and is empowered to resist violation. Instead of limitations being placed upon you to keep you from expansion and exploration, you get to set limits about who has access to you and how much. In the queendom, boundaries look less like fences or cages and more like skin, an organic substance that holds you together while keeping infection out so that you can roam safely about.

When Jesus says "Take up your cross," I think he means precisely that. Take up *your* cross, then stop. Don't try to carry two or six or five hundred. Don't hold on to crosses other people have slapped across your shoulders and told you to carry. Every life will inevitably contain suffering, but it's not about how much you carry. It is, as Mary Oliver says, "*how* you carry it." There is no prize for how *much* you can endure, and it is not the destiny of a strong woman that she must suffer loads.

TAKE UP YOUR CROSS, THEN STOP. DON'T TRY TO CARRY TWO OR SIX OR FIVE HUNDRED. DON'T HOLD ON TO CROSSES OTHER PEOPLE HAVE SLAPPED ACROSS YOUR SHOULDERS AND TOLD YOU TO CARRY.

Sister, there are times when you can lay that cross down and walk away. This business of voluntarily putting up with mistreatment is not of God. We do it in our homes, in our jobs, in our organizations, even in our friendships. We do not always have the option to leave, but if the option exists, why stay?

There is a time and place to enter into solidarity with another person's suffering. As I said in chapter 1, there is something quite humbling and even instructive about the image of a male Christ, of a God who willingly divests himself of power and allows himself to be crucified alongside us. But there is nothing inherently righteous about being crucified. Women are too often crucified for no other reason than to prop up the patriarchy. So if you can climb down from that cross, climb down!

Of course, women who climb down are usually vilified. Praising Jephthah's daughter is easy even for the patriarchy because she died. Regardless of how she may have resisted death, you can focus on her seeming compliance and leave it at that. But what if you're more like Delilah? She's the one in Judges 16 who helps the Philistines take down Samson, and I was always taught she was a seductress and a betrayer. But is that who she really was?

Samson, if you don't remember, is the last—and worst—of the Israelite judges. Everything about him is extreme. In terms of both strength and weakness, Samson comes across more like a caricature than a character. He is almost too powerful, too stupid, and too rash to be real. For example, he reportedly killed one thousand Philistines with the jawbone of a donkey. As for women, he treats them like property to which he is entitled. At one point in his story, he tries to return to his wife, whom he had abandoned, and demands to be let into her room. Her father is like, "I was so sure you hated her that I gave her to your best companion. But here, you can have her sister instead. She's prettier." This pisses Samson off, so he catches three hundred foxes (like you do when you're mad), ties them tail-to-tail with burning torches, and sets them loose in the fields of the Philistines.

BUT THERE IS NOTHING INHERENTLY RIGHTEOUS ABOUT BEING CRUCIFIED. WOMEN ARE TOO OFTEN CRUCIFIED FOR NO OTHER REASON THAN TO PROP UP THE PATRIARCHY.

Later in the story, he falls in love with Delilah. The Philistines, who've lost so many men to Samson's single-handed rage, tell Delilah that if she will help them capture Samson, they will give her eleven hundred pieces of silver. I'm not sure how long that kind of money would last, but it was a whole lot more than the thirty pieces Judas got. Delilah agrees to this plan, and she tries to coax Samson into telling her the secret of his strength. The first three times, he lies to her. How does she know he's lying? Because every time he gives her an answer, she tries taking away his strength, but it never works. How Samson didn't piece it together that she was trying to rid him of his strength, I do not know. Finally, on the fourth try, he gives in and tells Delilah the truth. She chops off his hair, the real secret to his strength, while he is sleeping, and the Philistines capture him.

She is the only woman in the latter half of Judges we know by name, and I was always taught that Delilah was bad. However, if her story were told from the perspective of the Philistines, Delilah would have been a hero who used what power she had to take down a tyrant. Even if we don't see her from the Philistine point of view, you have to admit she was persistent and resourceful.

HOW A WOMAN RESPONDS *TO* *ABUSE IS OFTEN* *MORE HARSHLY* *CRITICIZED THAN* *THE ABUSE ITSELF.*

The text says that Samson loved her, but the story never says whether Delilah loved Samson. We can make some guesses based on prior behavior about how Samson may have treated her, and it almost certainly wasn't with dignity. If she knew the fate of Samson's first wife (after Samson's terrible treatment of her, she was burned alive by the Philistines on account of the Samson/Philistine feud), Delilah had reason to be scared and reason to be cunning. For all we know, the Philistines' offer was not just about the money. It might have been her ticket to safety. Maybe she was sneaky *because she had to be.* She has been remembered and retold as one of the "bad girls of the Bible," but maybe she was just a woman who said "No more" to abuse, figured out a way to provide for herself, and left. Maybe Delilah was smart, brave, and boundaried.

I cannot think of a single time in my life when I have stood up to abuse and not been vilified, questioned, or critiqued for doing it. Women have a hard time setting boundaries not just because we were taught not to but also because we are punished, stalked, or maligned when we do. *How a woman responds to abuse is often more harshly criticized than the abuse itself.* I think this is because women are expected to bear crosses and bear them silently. It is a shock to the system when we set them down, name them as unjust, and refuse to carry them.

That flat-rock meditation I used to do? The one where I sat so "serenely" above my thoughts and feelings as they floated on by? That was before my divorce, when I was still trying to endure abuse and stay married. It was when I let myself feel and accept what was happening to me as real that I found the courage to lay that cross down and walk away. It wasn't my cross to bear, and I haven't missed it since.

CHAPTER 8

Mama God

In the opening chapter of Hosea, God asks his prophet Hosea to marry a promiscuous woman named Gomer as an example to the people of their own infidelity, and God gives Gomer's children these absolutely awful, cringeworthy names—names like *Jezreel*, to remind the people of massacre; *Lo-ruhamah*, meaning "not loved"; and *Lo-ammi*, meaning "you are not my people." (Just a few ideas if you happen to be looking for baby names and *Gomer* didn't immediately strike your fancy.)

The beginning of Hosea is not usually a go-to passage for feminists because God comes across like a stalking, violent husband who won't just let a woman leave. In 2019, I heard a remarkable sermon at Nevertheless She Preached on this very text by womanist scholar Dr. Wil Gafney. Dr. Gafney had the wits to draw our attention to chapter 1, verse 8, which says, "After she had weaned Lo-ruhamah, Gomer had another son."

"After Gomer had weaned her," Dr. Gafney repeated the line. *This child named* Not Loved *was fed at her mother's breast.*

This, said Dr. Gafney, is where God's presence shows up in the text, because no matter what God's people have done, no matter what the children are named, the mother-love of God cannot be contained—is compelled to pick this child up and provide nourishment. Even amid one of the harsher indictments of God's people by a prophet, the mother-love of God shines through. I was holding a foster baby on my hip as Dr. Gafney spoke, and the tears poured down my face. I could feel the mother-love of God pouring through me into this child, making sure that no matter what, she would not be left behind. It seemed to me that like the mother whose breasts leak milk when she hears her baby cry, the very body of God couldn't betray or abandon her creation.

IT IS NOT THAT FEMININE IMAGES OF THE DIVINE DO NOT EXIST IN SCRIPTURE AND IN CHRISTIANITY; IT'S THAT YOU HAVE TO TRAIN YOUR EYE TO SEE THEM AND YOUR EAR TO HEAR THEM BECAUSE THE PATRIARCHY HAS DONE EVERYTHING IT CAN TO DROWN HER VOICE OUT AND DISGUISE HER APPEARANCE.

Some readers might be so appalled by the way God shows up in Hosea chapter one that they would abandon this story altogether, but Dr. Gafney read the text with X-ray vision, taking us beyond the outerwear of the story and down to its bones, where the presence of God shows up most visibly not in condemnation but in the act of breastfeeding. Dr. Gafney engaged in what I would call a counter-reading of the text, the act of resisting the traditional understanding (i.e. "God is out to punish"), and read the text through the eyes of mother and child. This breastfeeding God shows up in Hosea once more in chapter 11 when God says, "It was I who taught Ephraim to walk, taking them by the arms; but they did not realize it was I who healed them. I led them with cords of human kindness, with ties of love. To them I was like one who lifts a little child to the cheek, and *I bent down to feed them.*"

In Isaiah 49, when the people feel that God has forgotten them, God replies, "Can a woman forget her nursing child, or show no compassion for the child of her womb?" he word used in the Bible to describe God's mercy and compassion comes from the root of the Hebrew word for womb. God cannot forget us because She is our Mother.

It is not that feminine images of the divine do not exist in Scripture and in Christianity; it's that you have to train your eye to see them and your ear to hear them because the patriarchy has done everything it can to drown Her voice out and disguise Her appearance. The way She surfaces in Hosea in the middle of an otherwise brutal story is how She often appears to us—peeking out from behind the shadows; showing up in dreams, in art, and in poetry; providing nourishment in the midst of desolation; making subtle but profound appearances that are easy enough to find if you're looking but easy enough to ignore if you prefer not to see. It is one of the ways She persists despite the continual onslaught of crucifixion—by being sly but consistent. The patriarchy may do everything in its power to envelope Her in a haze and obscure Her from view, but even after millennia of trying, no one has been able to erase Her. She persists.

Dr. Alicia Reyes-Barriéntez, a political scientist and *barrio* theologian, who was another speaker at Nevertheless She Preached, referred to God as "Mama Guad," a lovely reference to Our Lady of Guadalupe. In the story of Guadalupe, the Virgin Mary appears to Juan Diego on the hilltop of Tepeyac in 1531 and asks him to build a temple in her honor. He has to try three times before he succeeds in convincing the bishop to build the temple, but pilgrims still visit the site today. When Guadalupe appears to Juan Diego for a second time, she blesses him with these words:

Am I not here who am your Mother?
Are you not under my shadow and my protection?
Am I not your source of joy?
Are you not in the folds of my mantle,
And in the crossing of my arms?
Is there anything else you need?

I am reminded of a song written by my friend Rev. Fran Pratt:

In times of trouble, pain, and strife,
I know that God is near.
She holds me in the crook of her arm
And whispers of her love.

It is significant that Our Lady of Guadalupe appears to Juan Diego on the hill of Tepeyac because Tepeyac is the *same hill* where a temple to the Aztec mother goddess, or Earth Mother, Tonantzin, resided until it was destroyed by Catholic priests when the Spanish conquistadors arrived in Mexico. *Tonantzin* means "our sacred mother" in the Nahuatl language. It is as if Tonantzin found a way to resurrect or reincarnate herself in the form of Mary.

In her book *The Dance of the Dissident Daughter*, Sue Monk Kidd notes that "over the long course of church history, Mary had been the closest thing Christianity had to an archetype of the Feminine Divine. For many she filled the vacuum in the divine image . . ." Of course, Protestants have done a decent job of demoting her status, but Kidd describes an experience she had as a child and a Southern Baptist, spending the night at the home of a Catholic family. She came across a porcelain statue of Mary, and Kidd experienced "an inexplicable rush of feeling," what she interpreted as "the magnetic pull to the

Feminine Divine." Even in Christianity, a religion too often deprived of the Divine Feminine, the Great Mother has made an intractable appearance in the form of Mary.

As a mother myself, the image of the Divine Mother resonates deeply for me, and yet it would be a mistake to think of the divine feminine as mother only, as if She is limited to one type of role. But it is also a mistake to make *mother* itself a limiting image, as if *mother* means "meek" and *Mary* equals "mild." The book of Hosea also describes God like a mama bear whose cubs have been stolen. This Mama God is fiercely protective and ready to devour.

Mary, unlike the docile thing she has often been portrayed as in sermons and in art, must have been full of grit and gumption to survive all that she did—the scandal of being an unwed mother, the torture and death of her son, the risk to herself and her family. She has been painted into books and into picture frames, into cathedrals and into music as the ever-young, ever-so-innocent virgin. The moderns have interpreted *virgin* to be about sex, or, more accurately, the lack thereof, as if the non-act of virginity were some sort of noble feat favored by the gods. They imagine a surprise meeting between old, wise Gabriel and a naive little girl.

But in my imagination, she has never been young, and she has never been innocent. I think she was born an old soul, as if she came out of the womb grieving, carrying the stories of her ancestors. I imagine her as one of those rare birds who could sense from a young age the generational wounds of the past. To be virgin means to be whole, pure, and undivided. Being one who felt the conflicts of the ages warring inside her heart, Mary would never have guessed herself pure. She would have felt, instead, stained by the blood of her people—from the blood of Abel to the blood of Uriah, the blood of the Levite's concubine to the blood of the Canaanites. I imagine nothing about this alertness to pain felt pure to her.

But the heavens judged otherwise. They knew only someone such as this—one who had borne the agony of her people—could be ripe for conceiving heaven-sent, human-born hope. What if this is what is meant by the virgin birth?

THE GOD WHO BIRTHED THE WORLD CHOSE TO BE BORN IN MARY, CHOOSES TO BE BORN AGAIN AND AGAIN THROUGH WILLING HUMANS WHO CONCEIVE GOD AFRESH IN EACH GENERATION.

It has been said God needed a virgin to be born in. Maybe not an untouched female but an undistracted human being, untainted by self-deception. Someone who knew themselves and their world with open-eyed honesty. Someone with enough uncluttered space within themselves to grow the seed of God, available for swelling out with divine energy. I believe God still looks for such persons—male and female wombs that are fertile. Imagine that! The God who birthed the world chose to be born in Mary, chooses to be born again and again through willing humans who conceive God afresh in each generation.

Imagine! The magnificent divine choosing to come to us as vulnerable as an infant! Why? Because the divine was first a mother Herself, and as such, She cannot abandon Her creation. (I find it hard to imagine that any man would decide that the best way to help the world would be to show up in it as an utterly dependent baby. Some feminine creative spark must have been at work dreaming up the incarnation of Christ, a feminine energy that knew intimately the miraculous power of birth.) So She comes to us in human skin, small enough to cradle, so we will not just believe but sense and smell and see that we are not alone. This is God's great plan, to come to us disguised in the ordinary. I believe it is Her plan still. In the words of Clarissa Pinkola Estés, "In some hierarchies of the churchly kind, should any man, woman, or child say aloud that they travel with La Virgen on a regular basis—and wish to seek validation of that by the Roman Catholic Church—a group of assigned 'judges' will be dispatched to 'investigate,' to authenticate.' But meanwhile our Lady, Seat of Wisdom, seems to pay no attention. She keeps appearing without any authority's permission, without any institutional sanction, to those in need. She bypasses all gatekeepers, appointed or self-appointed, and instead flies to intervene, lift spirits, direct, heal, and liberate souls throughout the world."

Her rule-obliterating tenacity reminds me of the Spirit that falls upon Eldad and Medad in Numbers 11 even though Joshua tries to shut it down. In Hebrew, the word for "spirit" (*ruah*) is feminine.

Hopefully it is obvious to you by now, if it wasn't already, that *woman* is way more prevalent and more significant in Scripture than we have been led to believe. Part of the reason she has been so indistinct for us in the past is that the Bible has been written, translated, interpreted, read, and preached to us predominately by men.

I think of how my friends who are allergic to gluten seem to have developed a radar that is fine-tuned to notice any foods on the menu or at the table that might have gluten. I, on the other hand, have been consuming ignorantly all my life because I didn't feel the need to pay attention. It's not until I listen and understand the concerns of someone affected by celiac disease, for example, that I begin to notice gluten. Patriarchy is like that too. If it's not, say, actively damaging *your* intestines in any obvious way, you might not ever see it. And if you don't hear from and listen to women who preach, who interpret, who write, and who lead who *are* affected, you definitely won't see it. Keeping women from the pulpit and out of positions of power is the perfect way to ensure that almost no one sees. Even *other women* won't see it because their own reality is preached/described/ explained to them by men who cannot see.

For example, the book of Judges has one of the most diverse sets of female characters in the Bible, yet we are rarely encouraged to read it. If we do read it, we are conditioned to read it through the eyes of the men—Delilah is the bad one, not Samson; Jephthah is a man of faith, even though he murders his daughter. When I was exploring ministry as a college student, I was told by my male pastor that the only reason Deborah from Judges 4 served as a prophetess and judge is because no other men would step up to the role. The text doesn't say that; he added that interpretation on his own to protect male privilege.

I've already mentioned that the writer of Judges is setting readers up for the necessity of the monarchy as things grow increasingly worse throughout the book. This is especially true for the women. At the beginning of the book, we find some of the strongest women in all of Scripture—Achsah, Deborah, Jael. By the end, we find the most brutalized women in the Bible—the unnamed, dismembered concubine and the six hundred victims of rape that follow her. The plight of women declines dramatically, and the supposed solution to this mayhem and murder is a king who will lead the people. But a king turns out not to be a solution at all, *particularly if you read the story through the eyes of women.* You might say that these stories then further set us up for the necessity of Jesus, the messiah.

Let's talk a bit about the arrival of Jesus. There are only four women named explicitly in the genealogy of Jesus in Matthew 1 (although, obviously, none of the men in the lineup were getting born without women's bodies to bear them). In 2014, I decided to preach an Advent sermon series on the four women who are named in the genealogy: Tamar, Rahab, Ruth, and Bathsheba. The way I read Bathsheba's story in particular (which comes so soon after Judges), the need for Jesus was especially poignant.

In my retelling of Bathsheba's story, I imagine her coming to comfort Tamar, David's daughter, after Tamar has been raped by her half-brother, Amnon. Bathsheba is sympathetic, and as the two women talk, Bathsheba begins to tell of her own experience, relaying to this young woman what it had been like for her as a young woman, a wife, married to Uriah: How she had been bathing one day after her period, the ceremonial washing of the blood. How she always grieved when her period came, for it meant that yet again, she and Uriah were not with child. How she was still inwardly mourning the signs of her infertility when a messenger appeared at her door, inviting her to come see the king. How surprised she was, then alarmed—worried that perhaps Uriah had been wounded in battle or worse, killed. How she had hurried to the palace and was caught off guard by the king's friendly demeanor with her, how he didn't even act as if there was a war going on at all, how uncomfortable she felt, and how she had wished Uriah had been there because he might have known what to say to a king. How David was playful with her, how he took her on a tour of the palace under the guise of showing her around, how he took her into his chambers, how he lifted her skirts, how she was crying and trembling, but he did not notice. How she returned home, distraught and disheveled. How, to her horror, she later realized she was pregnant—and since her ritual bath had just occurred, she knew the child was David's, not Uriah's. How she didn't know what to do, couldn't imagine telling Uriah the truth about the king he so faithfully served. How she wasn't even sure if anyone would believe her, and if they did, would her life be in danger? How she wrote to the king out of desperation, telling him about the baby, hoping he would know to do. How the next thing she heard was that her husband had been killed in battle—only, she knew this was no war casualty How she was in shock that killing Uriah could possibly be David's version of "fixing it." How she blamed herself, wondering how things might have turned out if she had just never sent that letter. How after the time of mourning had passed, King David made a great show of welcoming Bathsheba, the poor widow of Uriah, into his house as his new wife. How the people had found it romantic. How she had felt despondent. How no one knew what really happened.

Tamar, of course, is in shock to learn the truth about her own father. But Bathsheba feels it was necessary to tell Tamar the story because Tamar has been feeling so tormented by the fact that her father has done nothing to protect her honor after being raped by her own brother. Bathsheba thinks David did nothing because "like father like son," and if he were to confront the evil in Amnon, he would have to own up to the evil within himself. She wants Tamar to know David's silence is not about her; it's about him. The two women lament together, saying, "If only we had a king willing to be ruined on behalf of the people."

THE SIGNIFICANCE OF THE MOTHER MARY IS NOT ONLY ABOUT SEEING HER AS A REPRESENTATION OF THE DIVINE FEMININE BUT ALSO ABOUT BEING ABLE TO SEE THE DIVINE REPRESENTED IN ALL OF US ORDINARY WOMEN, WHO, AS IT TURNS OUT, ARE CAPABLE OF BIRTHING GOD.

This is why I tell Tamar's story during my final Advent sermon the Sunday before Christmas; it highlights how the coming Christ would be a very different kind of king indeed. He would be the kind of man willing to be crucified, the kind of man more concerned with compassion than self-preservation. I do not wish to lose or diminish this piece ✓ of the Christian story. The kind of king Jesus chooses to be is tremendously significant. But I also want to suggest that there can be no more divorcing Jesus from his mother. Without her womb to birth him, Love Incarnate never makes it into the world.

Also, he wasn't an *actual* king. He had no power at all in the institutional sense. No crown. No throne. No scepter. No royal court. No servants. No wealth. No imperial subjects. (Jesus fits into the model of queendom quite well, thank you very much.)

When I read the genealogy of Jesus with X-ray vision, I see all the women—women who have been maligned, like Bathsheba, and women who are not even named—who made each birth in the chain possible. It seems to me that the significance of the Mother Mary is not only about seeing *her* as a representation of the divine feminine but also about being able to see the divine represented in all of us ordinary women, who, as it turns ✓ out, are capable of birthing God, of being the ancestors of the miraculous, and of hosting divinity in our bodies.

CHAPTER 9

Homecoming

Before the time of the kings, before Mary, before Jesus, right in Judges 1, we meet Achsah, a female landowner. She not only owns land in Negev; she has the audacity to ask her father for additional land with springs of water. She is described in derogatory fashion by one commentator as "the woman who wanted more," but actually I find "the woman who wanted more" to be a quite lovely epithet. Another male commentator calls her the "discontented wife," as if her capacity to name what she wanted was a bad thing. To that I say, if only more women would pay attention to their discontent! We would be so much faster to rise up. So much more likely to ask for what we deserve, need, and want, and therefore more likely to receive it. Achsah was a woman who asked for what she wanted and got it. Leave it to the male commentators to find something wrong with that.

Soon after the appearance of landowner Achsah and right before the appearance of Jael, mighty warrior, Judges gives us Deborah, who is both prophetess and judge. The Hebrew people come to her for words from God. She leads and directs and guides them, and no one seems to object based on her gender. Our English translations call her Deborah, "wife of Lappidoth," but that could also be translated as "woman of Lappidoth," noting where she is from rather than who she is married to. *Lappidoth* means "torch" and has the connotation of being fiery, so perhaps "woman of Lappidoth" means Deborah is a woman of fire.

In Judges 5, Deborah leads the people in song after a victory in battle, and in the song she names herself a "mother in Israel." We don't know if she had biological children or not, but she certainly mothered a nation into forty years of peace. Without her leadership, the people would not fight on their own behalf. She reports, "They held back until I, Deborah, arose, until I arose, a mother in Israel."

IF, AS A SOCIETY TODAY, WE FINALLY VALUED WOMEN AS EQUAL TO MEN, WE WOULDN'T BE MAKING HISTORY. WE WOULD BE RE-CREATING IT. WE WOULD BE RETURNING TO OUR ROOTS.

Achsah, Deborah, Jael: the strongest women in the book of Judges are at the *beginning* of the story. If, as a society today, we finally valued women as equal to men, we wouldn't be making history. We would be re-creating it. We would be returning to our roots.

Scholar Merlin Stone (drawing on the work of Professor Thorkild Jacobsen) points out that humanity's early, primeval belief in both female and male deities in heavenly assemblies likely reflected the reality on the ground—that is, women in leadership was the norm. What if the queendom is nothing new at all but a return to something very, very ancient?

The very institution of a kingdom was original to patriarchal religion. By contrast, the goddess religions *preceding* kingdoms were communally oriented and governed by assemblies instead of single rulers. Merlin Stone questions our modern treatment of monotheism as a more civilized or advanced type of religion, noting that polytheism may have symbolized a more communal attitude in society, whereas monotheism reflects "the political ideology that places all power in a single dominant person." What if, in the beginning, the tables were round, both on earth and in heaven?

What if the very Ground of Being Herself is not competitive but communal, not a power over but a power from within?

Retracing history to a handful of strong women in Judges doesn't even begin to scratch the surface of ancient feminine power. "At the very dawn of religion, God was a woman. Do you remember?" Merlin Stone asks in her groundbreaking book *When God Was a Woman*. With great attention to archeological evidence, Stone traces the history of goddess worship, demonstrating that in prehistoric and early historic times, societies often revered the goddess as the supreme deity and creator. Although she focuses her research on the Near and Middle East, she notes that female deities were worshipped in every part of the world. She explains that the earliest form of religion was likely one of ancestor worship. In prehistoric times, procreation was much more of a mystery than it is today, which is to say, people didn't realize men had anything to do with it! Thus mothers were often viewed as the sole parent. Understandably, ancient people traced their lineage through their mothers and grandmothers. And if a person or a culture imagined tracing back far enough

WHAT IF THE QUEENDOM IS NOTHING NEW AT ALL BUT A RETURN TO SOMETHING VERY, VERY ANCIENT?

to arrive at a first ancestor, naturally, she would have been a woman. Numerous sculptures of the female form, likely used in practices of worship, have been found in archeological digs across ancient Europe dating back as far as 25,000 BCE. If any miraculous force gave birth to the world, of course that force was female. Women, not men, gave birth; thus the source of all life, the creator, the supreme deity in ancient culture was female, and she was "supreme" not because she was a conqueror but because she was the first birth-giver. She was revered for her capacity to create life, not dominate it. By definition as the Mother of Life, she brought more people, more beings, more plants and animals to the table.

IF ANY MIRACULOUS FORCE GAVE BIRTH TO THE WORLD, OF COURSE THAT FORCE WAS FEMALE.

The reason we don't hear much or learn much about ancient goddess worship today is not because female deities gradually faded from society; they were pushed out. Goddesses and their devotees were hunted, hounded, stoned, burned, lectured, imprisoned, subjected to inquisitions, forced into hiding—for millennia. Stone demonstrates how in the ancient Middle East, goddess worship was violently attacked and suppressed by invading northerners. For evidence of her claim, we need look no further than the Bible, which records not only the massive conquest of the Canaanite people but a fierce effort to stamp out the indigenous religions.

Achsah was a strong woman and landowner, but it is important to note that her request for land *took place in the middle of a bloody land acquisition in Cana.* When she asked her father for land, she was asking for land that had been stolen from the Canaanites. When viewed fully in context, Achsah is less a heroine of female empowerment and more a prototype of white feminism, exemplifying for us the type of blind "empowerment" that is codependent with the colonial system. What I mean is, Achsah's personal advancement was built upon the subjugation of other people groups, including other women. As Audre Lorde famously said, "The master's tools will never dismantle the master's house." Achsah herself was a victim of the violent system, given in marriage as a prize to the man who attacked and captured the area of Kiriath Sepher. Her father, Caleb, appears to have ordered the attack on Kiriath Sepher unprovoked and for no other reason than to acquire their land, using Achsah like a pawn to inspire further conquest. Achsah attempted to better her own situation—desiring to *own* property, not *be* property—by asking for stolen lands.

What, I wonder, could she have done instead? Were alternative options available to her? Was there a way to rise above her own situation in such a way that more women could rise with her? I do not know. What I do know is how we must handle her story *now*—and others like hers—which is to acknowledge the full narrative, including the "prehistory" that is often overlooked and undertold. Let us not speak of Achsah without also remembering the Canaanite women who were subdued and stolen from before she arrived on the scene to claim "her" springs.

For us to return to the handful of strong women at the beginning of Judges is only barely scratching the surface of feminine power, not just because there were *so many more women* before them (and there were!), but also because the stories of women in the Bible take place *after* original goddess worship was already being silenced and suppressed. The Bible itself belongs to a religion that actively worked toward the obliteration of the feminine divine.

We cannot pretend the Bible is secretly a feminist document. The women who show up in Scripture as strong and independent often do so *in spite of* the religion that would otherwise hold them down, not because of it. We have to own this harrowing part of our narrative, our history, our legacy, or we simply cannot heal. That which remains suppressed and obscured can never be tended, amended, or transformed.

Can women find inspiration in Scripture? Of course! Can women find legitimate liberation themes in stories and passages from the Bible? Yes! But to act as if Scripture itself is unambiguously profemale erases its long history of damage to women.

WE CANNOT PRETEND THE BIBLE IS SECRETLY A FEMINIST DOCUMENT. THE WOMEN WHO SHOW UP IN SCRIPTURE AS STRONG AND INDEPENDENT OFTEN DO SO IN SPITE OF THE RELIGION THAT WOULD OTHERWISE HOLD THEM DOWN, NOT BECAUSE OF IT.

To me, it is simply not enough to return to the Bible and reread it through the eyes of women and recover the strong women whose stories are told there. That is surface-level feminism. To dismantle the patriarchy, we have to strip this house all the way down to the floorboards. We cannot just reclaim the gifts our faith instilled in us; we must also examine what injury our faith has done to the generations who came before, whose history and people and faith were harmed and silenced by its aggression.

Admittedly, this can be terrifying. Unpacking the patriarchal elements of Christianity might cause you to wonder if doing this work will inevitably lead to the loss of your faith altogether. I used to be afraid of this myself. What if deep digging led me not just beneath the surface but also into a tunnel that took me somewhere new entirely? What if I could no longer hold on to this Christianity that had been so important to me throughout my life? But as time passed, my priorities shifted. Digging deep became critical, essential, necessary. Holding on became less important. I felt increasingly ready to let go and find out what might catch me. Because wherever I land, that will be the truest place I've been so far.

Whether reading the Bible with honest eyes reinvigorates your faith or prompts you to look elsewhere for spiritual belonging, the process is *working*. Because the point isn't whether you go or remain inside the confines of a particular religion. It's whether you come alive. I believe holding on to a particular version of faith is far less important than keeping your integrity intact. Patriarchy kills, plain and simple. Your calling is to resurrect, to save your soul, to explore, and to become. Whether you stay or leave or leave then return is not really my concern, as long as you are becoming freer, fuller, braver, truthier, more alive, more awake, more fundamentally *who you are*.

Remember, the patriarchy has co-opted the value of staying into an absolute value so as to vilify anyone who leaves for any reason and for any amount of time. If alarm bells go off inside your head when you so much as step a foot over the fence or when you leave the kingdom for a daylong expedition or when you even just *imagine* the world beyond the village . . . ask yourself if those alarm bells sound from your deepest center or from your patriarchal conditioning. If the bells sound from your conditioning, see if, instead of silencing them, you can listen *beyond* them. There is always a deeper voice than the voice of your conditioning. I can't predict what it will say to you, but it might give you permission to transgress the boundary lines. It might tell you that you can fly. Or perhaps it will say, "Meet me back here tomorrow at noon. We've got work to do inside this kingdom. But until then, explore and have fun!"

> **PATRIARCHY KILLS, PLAIN AND SIMPLE. YOUR CALLING IS TO RESURRECT, TO SAVE YOUR SOUL, TO EXPLORE, AND TO BECOME.**

As you unreservedly explore your inner territory, it is important to remember that the thing you are discovering is not a new world to be conquered. You're discovering yourself! So I hope you treat her with reverence. If you try to impose the kingdom ways and the kingdom systems on your new discoveries, it's like colonizing yourself. Don't do that. Bring reverence and awe to the wild, original, primordial you. You may be leaving the patriarchal lands behind, but you are returning to yourself. It's less of a departure and more of a homecoming. It's like forfeiting one kind of world in order to save your own soul.

IN THE QUEENDOM, THERE IS ROOM FOR VARIATION, ROOM ENOUGH FOR MULTIPLE STORIES AND DISSENTING PERSPECTIVES, ROOM FOR THE FULL TRUTH OF OUR HISTORY—ITS LIBERATING ELEMENTS AND ITS OPPRESSIVE FORCES.

I'm not saying we all must hereby give up monotheism and Christianity. But I am suggesting we give up our patriarchal addiction to a singular, dominant narrative and a monolithic, dominant god. In the queendom, there is room for variation, room enough for multiple stories and dissenting perspectives, room for the full truth of our history—its liberating elements and its oppressive forces. In the queendom, we don't have to suppress alternative voices, whether those voices arise from a person on the margins or from within, speaking up from a marginalized area of the heart.

Long after the Hebrew invasion of Cana, as Christianity took hold in Western civilization and increased in influence, authorities continued to destroy sacred icons, idols, artifacts, and literature belonging to the pagan religions that predated them. Despite relentless attacks, the goddess continued to show up in many forms, often hiding in disguised spiritual practices deemed permissible by the conquerors. One notable example in Christianity is the way the divine feminine has persisted in the Mother Mary despite the church's concerted efforts to downplay her significance, as noted in the previous chapter. I just love how stubborn she is, don't you? It's as if she views being relegated to the margins as an opportunity to rise, to subvert, to innovate, to persist.

Despite the fact that worshipping the Goddess was increasingly forbidden by the Christian church, people continued their devotion to Her anyway, finding in the Mother Mary a timely substitute, turning their statues of Isis nursing her baby into images of the Madonna and child. If you trace the origins of the "Catholic" rosary, the practice developed from the circle of flowers people used to weave for the Goddess. In their book *The Way of the Rose*, Clark Strand and Perdita Finn write,

> The rosary was a way of grafting devotion to the Virgin onto the rootstock of far older, more earth-centered forms of goddess worship handed down from prehistoric times. When medieval people called out to Mary, they knew she wasn't just the mother of Jesus, as the Church would have them believe, but their mother from the bottom of time. She was with them before the beginning and after the end. She was called the Mother of Life, the Star of the Sea, the Queen of Heaven and Earth. These were the very same words of praise their ancestors had used to address Inanna, Isis, and Venus. Again and again, religious authorities leveled the sacred groves of the Mother to make way for churches and cathedrals. And they forbid the old prayers and practices. But people would not give up their devotion to her.

It strikes me how much Her capacity to persist was directly tied to the people's yearning to revere Her despite all threats and all conquest. It was a joint endeavor, this persistence. Like a partnership (not a lordship), like a creative act (not a domination), like a dance.

And today, when you and I return to the women in Scripture and reread their stories with fresh and feminist eyes, I believe we are engaging in the sacred work of keeping the divine feminine alive. We become participants in Her continual resurrection despite all patriarchal attempts to keep Her down, and in so doing, we also resurrect ourselves. The story of the divine feminine and of Her queendom is not distant and removed from our own lives; rather, Her story is our story, and in Her, we find ourselves.

We find ourselves in the pregnant virgin, giving birth to God in the world. We find ourselves in the battered concubine, beaten down when we try to speak our truth. We find ourselves in the resurrected Christa who defies defeat. We find ourselves in the landscape of Mother Earth as we explore our own inner territory, welcoming each bend in the river and each rise in the mountain. We find ourselves in the boldness of Jael as we grow and adapt to face new challenges. We find ourselves in the ingenuity of Jephthah's daughter, who fought to preserve time for herself as time was running out. We find ourselves in the Divine Mother, whose love is abundant and nonpossessive. We find ourselves in the ancient Goddess, whose original divinity can never be erased.

THE STORY OF THE DIVINE FEMININE AND OF HER QUEENDOM IS NOT DISTANT AND REMOVED FROM OUR OWN LIVES; RATHER, HER STORY IS OUR STORY, AND IN HER, WE FIND OURSELVES.

My hope for the future is that we will live our way back to a time when we no longer have to be subversive in our worship of Her; when She no longer needs to stay hidden in plain sight; when, as women, we no longer have to fight so damn hard just to be heard or seen; when our daughters are more empowered than our mothers could ever have imagined; when our ancient ancestors can sigh from their graves, "Aw, She's back in full force. Now I can rest in peace."

Let us pray together:

> Our Mother, who art in heaven,
> Hallowed be thy name,
> Thy Queendom come,
> Thy love be revealed,
> On earth as it is in heaven.
> Give us this day, our daily bread.
> Forgive us the proclivity to exert power over,
> Liberate us with power from within.
> And lead us not into temptation,
> But deliver us from evil,
> For this is your Queendom,
> Where power and glory are shared. Amen.

Acknowledgments

First I want to acknowledge my teachers, beginning with Dr. Marty Alan Michelson, my first professor of Hebrew Scripture, who opened my imagination to the interpretive possibilities of working with Scripture. Dr. Michelson also introduced me to Jason Hubbert, who wrote a graduate thesis titled "From Hero to Whore: A Study of the Portrayal of Women in the Book of Judges" (he tells me he would title it differently now using language other than *whore*), which he shared with my undergraduate class. His work deeply impacted me and has stayed with me ever since, resulting in a lifelong fascination with the women in Judges. I am deeply indebted as well to my professors of Hebrew Bible in seminary, Dr. Dennis Tucker and most especially Dr. Lai Ling Ngan. Dr. Ngan was the only woman of color in my entire theological education, and she also happened to be the best teacher I ever had. It was she who introduced me to feminist biblical interpretation, and because of her, I had my first encounter with Phyllis Trible's seminal work *Texts of Terror*, another significant influence in my understanding of women in the Bible, particularly in the book of Judges. I am also grateful for the artwork of Kevin "Kevissomo" Rolly and his project *In the Time of the Judges* as well as the artwork of Lisbeth Cheever-Gessaman.

ACKNOWLEDGMENTS

Huge thanks to Rev. Aurelia Dávila Pratt for volunteering to be the "captain of my cheer squad" and seriously being my cheerleader in everything for the last ten years. I am deeply grateful to the community of Nevertheless She Preached for being a place of great hope for myself and for women around the world and to Rev. Natalie Webb for dreaming it up alongside me and making the dream a reality. I am grateful to Alivia Kate Stehlik for her unwavering support and to my kids, Leila and Kernada, a.k.a. "Blakely," for the best snuggles and smiles a mom could ever want.

Thanks to all the people who believe in me, which is too many to name, but I do want to give a shout-out to a few of you for being especially persistent: Sharyl, Sarah, Jessica, Hayley, Rhonda, Jill. Thanks to Rev. Emmy Kegler for connecting me to Lisa Kloskin at Broadleaf Books and to Broadleaf Books for helping bring my book to fruition! I also want to thank some of my teachers who I only know by their writings—Sue Monk Kidd, Clarissa Pinkola Estés, and Toko-pa Turner, to name just a few. I acknowledge also all the women—too many of them unknown and unnamed—who so bravely forged this path, making my life and my knowing and my liberation possible. Who made our liberation possible.

Notes

CHAPTER 1

1 **"My Lord Moses, stop them!":** Numbers 11:28.

2 **"Are you jealous for my sake? . . . would put his spirit on them!":** Numbers 11:29.

4 **"If God is man, then man is God.":** Mary Daly, *Beyond God the Father: Toward a Philosophy of Women's Liberation* (Boston: Beacon Press, 1973), 19.

6 **A 2020 study by the UN Development Programme:** Liz Ford, "Nine out of 10 People Found to Be Biased against Women," *Guardian*, March 5, 2020, https://tinyurl.com/yx8wfy4s.

7 **"desecrating our symbols":** Jon White, "'Christa' on Display at St. John the Divine," Episcopal Café, October 5, 2016, https://www.episcopalcafe.com/38546-2/.

10 **"Did you want to see me broken? . . . But still, like air, I'll rise.":** Maya Angelou, "Still I Rise" in *And Still I Rise: A Book of Poems* (New York: Random House, 1978).

11 **Dr. Ada Maria Isasi-Diaz, mother of mujerista theology:** Dr. Ada Maria Isasi-Diaz first heard the word kin-dom from the Franciscan nun, Georgene Wilson. Dr. Isasi-Diaz later wrote, "Kin-dom of God: A Mujerista Proposal," an important critique and revisioning of the kingdom of God.

12 **archeological evidence suggests the matrilineal, goddess-worshipping societies . . . :** Merlin Stone, *When God Was a Woman* (New York: Harcourt, 1976).

16 **"Our Mother, who art in heaven, . . . Where power and glory are shared. Amen.":** Adapted from a feminine version of the Lord's Prayer given to me by Dr. Emma J. Church.

CHAPTER 2

17 **"Here is my virgin daughter and his concubine. . . . do whatever you want to them.":** Judges 19:23–25 (my translation).

18 **Only six hundred men escaped:** Judges 20.

19 **they gave the remaining four hundred virgins to the lonely Benjamites:** Judges 21:12.

19 **next they abducted two hundred women from Shiloh:** Judges 21:19–23.

19 **Bathsheba . . . was merely minding her own business when David summoned her to his quarters to sleep with her:** 2 Samuel 11.

20 **In response, David did nothing:** 2 Samuel 13.

21 **when you become a foster parent, you are entering into a delicate and complicated system:** I want to acknowledge here that racial dynamics are often at play in foster care, where white foster parents are hailed as the saviors of Black and brown children, and brown and Black biological parents can be unfairly targeted by the system. One particularly horrific example is when the children of deported immigrants are taken from their parents and placed in foster homes in the United States.

25 **"God has brought down rulers from their thrones. . . . has sent the rich away empty.":** Luke 1:52–53.

25 **"every valley shall be raised up, every mountain and hill be made low":** Isaiah 40:4.

25 **Mary's song appears:** Luke 3:5.

27 **The "heart is deceitful above all things, and desperately wicked,":** Jeremiah 17:9 KJV.

29 **"If the first woman God ever made was strong enough . . . the men better let them.":** There is some debate about the accuracy of this quotation. To read the full speech or for more information, visit "Sojourner Truth (1797–1883): Ain't I a Woman?," speech delivered at the Women's Convention, Akron, Ohio, December 1851, Modern History Sourcebook, https://tinyurl.com/jjooldv.

CHAPTER 3

37 **"We are taught to 'rise above' things like anger, anxiety, sadness . . . but from the magnificent spectrum of life itself.":** Toko-pa Turner, *Belonging: Remembering Ourselves Home* (Salt Spring Island, British Columbia: Her Own Room Press, 2017), 106.

41 **"The hero or heroine in mythical tales . . . who she is outside the expectations of the kingdom.":** Turner, 30.

44 **I'm currently taking an antiracism course:** Dr. Frantonia Pollins, "The Evil Behind Your Love and Light," online course featuring Rebekah Borucki, Dr. Rocio Rosales Meza, CiCi Gunn, Ashleyann Jones, Chrissy King, Nzingah Oniwosan, Dr. Darnise Martin, and Yeye Luisah Teish. July–August 2020.

48 *must* **get in touch with his anima:** For further reading on the topic of the anima energy in men, you might consider James Hollis's *Under Saturn's Shadow: The Wounding and Healing of Men* (Toronto: Inner City Books, 1994). For further reading on the balancing of anima and animus energy, see Turner, *Belonging*, or the work of Clarissa Pinkola Estés or the work of Pat McCabe, also known as Weyakpa Najin Win (Womaning Standing Shining).

48 **nonnegotiable for the healing of both the soul and the world:** I am deeply indebted to Rick Putman and Sheila Petruccelli and

their joint lectures on masculine spirituality as well as the Haden Institute for this insight.

CHAPTER 4

51 **"The Lord bless you, my son!":** Judges 17:2 NIV.

51 **"In those days there was no king in Israel; all the people did what was right in their own eyes.":** Judges 17:6.

51 **"Stay with me, and be to me a father . . . your living.":** Judges 17:10.

52 **"Now I know that the Lord will prosper me . . . my priest.":** Judges 17:13.

52 **"The Israelites again did what was evil *in the sight of the Lord.*":** Judges 3:12; 4:1; 10:6; 13:1 (emphasis added).

53 **"Go in peace. The mission you are on is *under the eye of the Lord.*":** Judges 18:6 (emphasis added).

53 **"they observed the people . . . and possessing wealth.":** Judges 18:7.

53 **"Is it better for you to be priest . . . to a tribe and clan in Israel?":** Judges 18:19.

53 **"having taken what Micah had made . . . and burned down the city.":** Judges 18:27.

54 **the same exact line with which the book ends:** Judges 21:25.

56 **When Judges 17 claims that "all the people did what was right in their own eyes,":** Judges 17:6.

56 **"heart is deceitful above all things, and desperately wicked.":** Jeremiah 17:9 KJV.

59 **The narrator says quite often, "There was no king in Israel.":** Judges 17:6; 18:1; 19:1; 21:25.

61 **"This being human is a guest house. / . . . as a guide from beyond.":** Used with permission. Coleman Barks, *The Illuminated Rumi* (New York: Broadway Books, 1997), 77.

CHAPTER 5

63 **the eleven nominate two men we readers have never heard of before:** Acts 1:14–26.

63 **"It was Mary Magdalene, Joanna, Mary the mother of James, and the other women . . . they did not believe them.":** Luke 24:10–11.

64 **he went away wondering to himself what had happened:** Luke 24:12–13.

64 **In Luke's account, it isn't until Jesus appears to the two travelers . . . that the story starts to gain credibility:** Luke 24:13–35.

65 **Jesus once cast seven demons out of her, and it doesn't say it was a demon of prostitution:** Mark 16:9.

66 **when she encounters the risen Christ alone in the garden:** John 20:11–18.

72 **"Sister, we know that the Savior greatly loved you . . . perhaps have never heard.":** Translation from Lynn Bauman, Ward Bauman, and Cynthia Bourgeault, *The Luminous Gospels* (Telephone, TX: Praxis Institute, 2008), as quoted in Cynthia Bourgeault, *The Meaning of Mary Magdalene: Discovering the Woman at the Heart of Christianity* (Boston: Shambhala, 2010).

72 **"Say what you will about all that she has said to us . . . from the rest of his teachings.":** Bourgeault, *Meaning of Mary Magdalene*, 75.

72 **"Would the Savior speak these things to a woman . . . more worthy than we are?":** Bourgeault, 76.

72 **"You have always been quick to anger, Peter. . . . If the Savior considered her worthy. . . . We should be ashamed. . . . he himself did not give us.":** Bourgeault, 76.

73 **"After Levi had said this, they departed . . . proclaiming the Good News.":** Bourgeault, 76.

74 **The Hebrew and Syriac claim she played the harlot, while the Greek and Old Latin say she became angry and left:** Phyllis

Trible, *Texts of Terror: Literary-Feminist Readings of Biblical Narratives* (Minneapolis: Fortress, 1984), 66.

75 **"The words 'speak to her heart' connote reassurance, comfort, loyalty, and love.":** Trible, 67.

76 **"Get up; let's go.":** Judges 19:28.

76 **"Has such a thing ever happened . . . take counsel, and speak out.":** Judges 19:30.

76 **the word *consider* is a translation of the Hebrew idiom "Direct to the heart,":** Trible, *Texts of Terror*, 81.

80 **murder conviction and about the various accusations of sexual assault and harassment against him:** Rod Aydelotte, "'Murdering Minister' Sentenced to 65 Years," NBC News, January 21, 2010, https://tinyurl.com/y9bwt2pc.

80 **a column in *Texas Monthly* from 2008:** Skip Hollandsworth, "The Valley of the Shadow of Death," *Texas Monthly*, March 2008, https://tinyurl.com/y73hnv25.

CHAPTER 6

87 **the spirit of God comes upon Jephthah *before* he makes this absurd vow:** Judges 11:29–30.

87 **"I am devastated. I have made a vow to the Lord that I cannot break,":** Judges 11:35.

87 **he doesn't explain why he can't break the vow:** Judges 11:35.

87 **I often imagine the mother of this young girl . . . even though the text leaves her out:** In 2010, the first time I preached on this text, Dr. Angela Reed approached me afterward, saying she wonders, "Where was her mother?" Dr. Reed's question has haunted me ever since.

88 **Like the ram for Isaac, she begs for a ram:** In Genesis 22, Abraham takes his son Isaac to a mountain to sacrifice him to God, but at the last minute, an angel of the Lord stops him, and there,

caught in a thicket, is a ram that Abraham uses instead of sacrificing his son.

89 **she takes a tent stake and drives it into his head:** Judges 4:17–22.

89 **takes Goliath's sword and chops off his head:** 1 Samuel 17:51.

90 **The person who defeated Goliath . . . was promised . . . great wealth:** 1 Samuel 17:25.

90 **she gave him milk and covered him with a blanket:** Judges 4:19.

91 **"the son of another woman.":** Judges 11:2.

91 **to Jephthah's surprise, they turn to him for help:** Judges 11:4–11.

92 **God . . . does not even show up for that conversation because no such bargaining is necessary:** Judges 4:30–31.

93 **"The saint who thinks he casts no shadow is very dangerous.":** Alan W. Jones, *Soul Making: The Desert Way of Spirituality* (New York: HarperOne, 1989), 37.

94 **"I think about these things often. . . . at the age when we went to Oxford.":** John Mortimer, *Clinging to the Wreckage* (London: Penguin, 1982), 222, as quoted by Jones, *Soul Making*, 38.

98 **"The Lord relented and did not bring on his people the disaster he had threatened.":** Exodus 32:14 NIV.

CHAPTER 7

104 **"Give me two months to roam the hills and weep with my friends, because I will never marry.":** Judges 11:37 NIV.

107 **"From this comes the Israelite tradition . . . to commemorate the daughter of Jephthah the Gileadite.":** Judges 11:39–40.

107 **"nevertheless she became a tradition.":** Trible, *Texts of Terror*, 106.

111 **killed one thousand Philistines with the jawbone of a donkey:** Judges 15:16.

111　**catches three hundred foxes . . . sets them loose in the fields of the Philistines:** Judges 15:4–6.

111　**he falls in love with Delilah:** See Judges 16.

CHAPTER 8

115　**God gives Gomer's children these absolutely awful, cringe-worthy names:** Hosea 1:2–9.

115　**God comes across like a stalking, violent husband:** See Hosea 2.

115　**In 2019, I heard a remarkable sermon:** Wil Gafney, "Nevertheless Gomer Persisted: Hosea 1:1–6," Nevertheless She Preached Conference, Monday, September 24, 2018, University Baptist Church, Waco, Texas.

115　**"After she had weaned Lo-ruhamah, Gomer had another son.":** Hosea 1:8 NIV.

116　**"It was I who taught Ephraim to walk . . . and I *bent down to feed them*.":** Hosea 11: 3–4 NIV (emphasis added).

117　**"Can a woman forget her nursing child, or . . . the child of her womb?":** Isaiah 49:15.

117　**Dr. Alicia Reyes-Barriéntez, a political scientist and barrio theologian:** Dr. Alicia Reyes-Barriéntez, "A White Jesus Can't Save a Brown Child: Unabridged Version," Nevertheless She Preached Conference, September 24, 2019, First Austin, Austin, Texas.

118　**"Am I not here who am your Mother? / . . . Is there anything else you need?":** Clark Strand and Perdita Finn, *The Way of the Rose: The Radical Path of the Divine Feminine Hidden in the Rosary* (New York: Penguin Random House, 2019), 21.

118　**"In times of trouble, pain, and strife, / . . . And whispers of her love.":** Used with permission. Fran Pratt, "Mother God Refrain," July 23, 2020, Outpost Press.

118　**"over the long course of church history":** Sue Monk Kidd, *The Dance of the Dissident Daughter: A Woman's Journey from*

Christian Tradition to the Sacred Feminine (New York: Harper-Collins, 1996), 40.

119 **This Mama God is fiercely protective and ready to devour:** Hosea 13:8.

121 **"In some hierarchies of the churchly kind.":** Clarissa Pinkola Estés, *Untie the Strong Woman: Blessed Mother's Immaculate Love for the Wild Soul* (Boulder, CO: SoundsTrue, 2011), 181, 184.

CHAPTER 9

127 **to ask her father for additional land with springs of water:** Judges 1:14–15.

127 **"wife of Lappidoth,":** Judges 4:4.

128 **"until I, Deborah, arose, until I arose, a mother in Israel.":** Judges 5:7 NIV.

128 **Scholar Merlin Stone points out that . . . women in leadership was the norm:** Stone, *When God Was a Woman*, 131.

129 **"the political ideology that places all power in a single dominant person.":** Stone, 131.

129 **"At the very dawn of religion, God was a woman. Do you remember?":** Stone, 1.

130 **look no further than the Bible, which records . . . a fierce effort to stamp out the indigenous religions:** See in particular the book of Joshua, which directly precedes Judges.

131 **Achsah herself was a victim of the violent system, given in marriage as a prize . . . :** Judges 1:12.

135 **origins of the "Catholic" rosary . . . the circle of flowers people used to weave for the Goddess:** Strand and Finn, *Way of the Rose*, 3–4.

135 **"The rosary was a way of grafting devotion . . . would not give up their devotion to her.":** Strand and Finn, 4–5.